· JUST FOR ONE ·

·JUST FOR ONE·

KATHARINE BLAKEMORE

This edition first published 1988 by
Hamlyn Publishing Group
Michelin House
81 Fulham Road
London SW3 6RB

© 1986 Hennerwood Publications Ltd.

ISBN 0 600 55881 9

Printed in Hong Kong

· CONTENTS ·

INTRODUCTION

Many people in modern society frequently find themselves preparing a meal just for one. Yet most recipes are written for four people or more, and recipe quantities cannot be scaled down to one quarter economically and efficiently. In this book, however, the reverse is possible and almost all the recipes can be doubled or quadrupled to feed two or four people when entertaining.

Many single cooks feel that experimenting with tempting new recipes simply is not worth the bother, hence their traditional dependence on tried and tested – but monotonous – favourites or on convenience pre-packaged foods. Although relatively little preparation is needed for convenience dishes, they can often take longer to cook than many of the recipes in this book – a

far from satisfactory situation for single gourmets with a discriminating taste.

Here is a book that capitalizes on and actually exploits the advantages of cooking for one.

Single cooks are probably the only sector of the population for whom, sometimes, it makes economic sense to buy the more expensive and quicker cooking cuts of meat. Cheaper cuts need longer to cook, often more preparation and many additional ingredients to enhance them, so that buying a cheaper cut can often work out more expensive than buying a chop or small piece of steak. Of course, not all the recipes in this book are based on expensive cuts of meat. In fact, there is a whole chapter devoted to vegetarian recipes, as well as many economical recipes based on eggs and cheese.

Shopping, planning and storing

It is important when cooking for one to plan and shop prudently. Never feel intimidated by asking for small amounts in butchers, fishmongers and greengrocers. Many supermarkets and greengrocers now have a 'choose your own' section for fruit and vegetables where you can not only buy just as much as you need, but also pick the best quality. If you are buying something that is not going to be used for a few days, choose underripe produce.

If you have to buy vegetables in larger quantities or have to buy a lot of food in advance, then storage is very important. Potatoes and other root vegetables should be kept in a cool, dark place. Salad vegetables should be kept in polythene bags in the salad drawer of a refrigerator. Meat and fish should not be bought too far in advance if possible. Take it out of its original wrappings, put it on to a plate, cover it with cling film and keep refrigerated.

Eggs should be stored at a constant temperature in a cool place, ideally between 7-13°C (45-55°F). If you do not have such a place, store eggs in the least cool part of the refrigerator. But bring them to room temperature before use, especially if they are to be separated and the egg whites whisked: you will find that the white will whisk more easily and have a larger volume if whisked at room temperature.

Try to plan menus ahead as much as possible, so that if only half a certain item is used for one meal, the remainder can be incorporated in another, thus avoiding waste, a common problem when cooking for one.

Wine and cream

In a few of the recipes wine and cream are used; this is not as extravagant as it might seem as both ingredients lift a dish out of the ordinary, and why shouldn't we spoil ourselves occasionally? Where single cream is specified, this can, in most cases, be substituted with the top of the milk. The best way to buy double or whipping cream for one person is to buy it frozen. It comes in small pieces or sticks and you can take out only as much as you need. You have to remember to defrost it, although in some savoury dishes the cream can be added frozen to the sauce, and then heated and melted gently.

It is not practical to buy a whole bottle of wine when only a small amount is needed for a recipe, but wine nowadays can be bought in small containers just big enough for one. Wine can now be bought in cans, cartons and individual bottles. Use whatever is necessary for the recipe and enjoy the rest with the meal! Wine boxes, although initially pricey, are a very good buy. The wine in them keeps well, so that you can use as little as you need.

After a party small amounts of wine are often left in bottles. This wine can be frozen in ice-cube trays, then transferred to polythene bags and used as required.

Store-cupboard ingredients

It is important for single cooks to keep a store-cupboard of frequently used ingredients. Herbs and spices are very important as flavourings for food, so do keep a supply of the most popular ones. Spices that you are likely to use frequently include nutmeg, cinnamon, paprika, cayenne pepper, cloves and allspice. They should be as fresh as possible. Buy them whole and grind them when you need them, or buy from an Indian shop where they are often freshly ground by the owners and can be bought in small quantities. Throughout the summer most garden centres and some greengrocers stock pots of fresh herbs such as parsley, dill, mint, basil, thyme, chives and marjoram. If you do not have a garden to transplant them into, they can be kept in the kitchen on a sunny windowsill. A mixture of chopped dried herbs such as thyme, savory, marjoram and oregano is invaluable during the winter, when many fresh herbs may not be readily available.

Some vegetables are very good canned. Canned tomatoes are an absolute necessity for any store-cupboard; other good canned vegetables are sweetcorn and flageolets (a small green bean with a very delicate flavour which is wonderful with lamb). Canned fish is very good as a standby: salmon, sardines, and tuna fish in particular are very versatile and can be served with salads, made into a pâté and used in a variety of hot dishes.

Dry ingredients such as lentils, pasta and rice are useful to have as they keep well. Look out for the small brown lentils de Puy from France; these have a lovely nutty flavour and stay whole when cooked. There are many varieties of rice available but one that I would recommend for all Indian and Middle Eastern influenced dishes is Basmati rice. It needs to be well washed and soaked before use, but has a short cooking time and a wonderful aroma and flavour. If it is not available, I recommend American long-grain, easy-cook rice as this is almost foolproof to cook: it needs only double the quantity of water to rice, a little salt and about 20 minutes cooking time.

Dried pasta is available in many shapes and sizes and is the basis for a variety of quick economical meals. Also look out for fresh pasta which is becoming more and more available. It keeps for only 2-3 days in the refrigerator but can be frozen. However, the main advantage of fresh pasta is that it takes only about 3 minutes to cook. Other ingredients useful for the store-cupboard are tomato purée, for one person best bought in a tube so that just the odd teaspoon can be used, and mango chutney for serving with Indian-type dishes and with cold meats. Bottled lemon juice, although not as good as fresh lemon juice, is useful when only one or two teaspoons of lemon juice are called for. Nuts are also a very useful addition to a store-cupboard; they can be bought in small packets in supermarkets and health food shops and can add an interesting texture and protein to many dishes.

Using the oven

Some of the recipes in this book require the use of the oven. At first this may seem uneconomical for one person; the answer is to consider what else the oven can be used for at the same time: a tray of biscuits or a small cake for example. Accompanying vegetables are often very good cooked in foil in the oven with the main course.

Equipment

There are certain items of equipment that I consider essential in any kitchen: a set of scales and measuring spoons, sharp knives, wooden spoons, a pair of scissors and a selection of pans of various sizes.

A small electric hand whisk is very useful, as is a small blender or liquidizer for making soups and sauces. If you are a very enthusiastic cook, then you might consider a small food processor.

If you intend to bake, a mixing bowl will be necessary as well as a few cake tins, perhaps one round and one loaf-shaped, together with a baking sheet and a cooling tray.

Whatever you decide to make from this book, you will find that preparation is kept simple, especially with the single cook in mind. All the recipes use trouble-free, readily available ingredients, many of which you will already have in your store-cupboard. You'll find that the delicious results will make cooking just for one a worthwhile pleasure.

SOUPS, SALADS AND SNACKS

• JERUSALEM ARTICHOKE AND • WATERCRESS SOUP ✓

25 g (1 oz) butter
225 g (8 oz) Jerusalem artichokes, peeled and chopped
1 small bunch watercress, stalks removed
1 leek, washed and sliced
200 ml (7 fl oz) chicken stock
85 ml (3 fl oz) milk
salt
freshly ground black pepper
To garnish:
1 sprig watercress

Preparation time: 15 minutes
Cooking time: 30 minutes

1. Melt the butter in a medium pan and add the artichokes, watercress and sliced leek. Stir well, cover the pan and cook for 10 minutes.
2. Add the stock, milk, salt and pepper, bring to the boil and simmer for 20 minutes.
3. Purée the mixture in a blender or pass through a sieve.
Ⓐ Ⓕ Reheat gently and serve garnished with the watercress sprig.

Ⓐ The soup can be made 1 day in advance, if covered and chilled.
Ⓕ Freeze for up to 3 months. Defrost overnight in the refrigerator or for 4-6 hours at room temperature.

• WELSH CAWL •

175 g (6 oz) lamb fillet
2 teaspoons oil
1 small leek, washed and sliced
1 small onion, peeled and chopped
300 ml (½ pint) beef stock
salt
freshly ground black pepper
1 small carrot, peeled and grated
1 small parsnip, peeled and grated
50 g (2 oz) swede, peeled and grated
To garnish:
1 teaspoon chopped parsley

Preparation time: 15 minutes
Cooking time: 45 minutes

1. Cut the lamb into small pieces. Heat the oil in a medium pan and add the lamb, leek and onion. Cook until brown.
2. Add the stock, salt and pepper to the pan, bring to the boil and simmer for 30 minutes.
3. Add the carrot, parsnip and swede to the pan and cook for a further 10 minutes. Ⓐ Ⓕ
4. Serve sprinkled with the chopped parsley.

Ⓐ The cawl can be made 1 day in advance, if covered and chilled.
Ⓕ Freeze for up to 3 months. Defrost overnight in the refrigerator or for 4-6 hours at room temperature. Reheat in a pan.

By using fillet of lamb, which is very tender, and grating the root vegetables, the cooking time is reduced considerably. Traditionally the broth was served first, followed by the meat and vegetables.

• SAUSAGE AND SWEETCORN • CHOWDER

2 teaspoons oil
100 g (4 oz) chipolata sausages
1 small onion, peeled and chopped
1 small potato, peeled and diced
½ × 198 g (7 oz) can sweetcorn
1 × 227 g (8 oz) can tomatoes, chopped and juice reserved
85 ml (3 fl oz) chicken stock
¼ teaspoon dried basil
salt
freshly ground black pepper

Preparation time: 10 minutes
Cooking time: 30 minutes

1. Heat the oil in a pan and cook the sausages until brown.
Ⓐ Remove from the pan with a slotted spoon or tongs.
2. Add the onion to the pan and fry until softened, then add the potato, sweetcorn, tomatoes and juice, stock, basil, salt and pepper. Bring to the boil and simmer for 20 minutes.
3. Slice the sausages and return to the pan. Reheat until the sausages are heated through. Serve immediately.

Ⓐ The sausages can be cooked 2-3 hours in advance and stored, covered, in a refrigerator.

ABOVE: Sausage and sweetcorn chowder; BELOW: Jerusalem artichoke and watercress soup

• CHICKEN PILAFF WITH LEMON • AND MINT

1 × 150 g (5 oz) boned chicken breast, skinned
15 g (½ oz) butter
1 small onion, peeled and chopped
1 garlic clove, peeled and chopped
½ teaspoon ground turmeric
1 teaspoon ground cumin
50 g (2 oz) Basmati rice, well washed
150 ml (¼ pint) chicken stock
2 teaspoons lemon juice
½ teaspoon dried mint
salt
freshly ground black pepper
To garnish:
slices of lemon
sprigs of fresh mint

Preparation time: 10 minutes
Cooking time: 15 minutes

1. Cut the chicken breast into strips. Melt the butter in a pan and fry the onion, garlic and chicken together until lightly browned.
2. Add the turmeric and cumin to the pan and cook for a further 3 minutes, stirring frequently.
3. Place the rice in the pan, then add the chicken stock, lemon juice, dried mint, salt and pepper. Bring to the boil, reduce the heat to low, cover the pan and cook for 10-12 minutes, or until the rice is tender and has absorbed all the liquid. Garnish the pilaff with the lemon slices and fresh mint, and serve.

• STUFFED GLOBE ARTICHOKE •

1 globe artichoke
salt
1 hard-boiled egg
25 g (1 oz) cooked ham
1 tablespoon mayonnaise
2 teaspoons chopped fresh parsley
salt
freshly ground black pepper
To garnish:
flat-leaved parsley sprig

Preparation time: 10 minutes, plus cooling
Cooking time: 35-40 minutes

1. Cut the base of the artichoke so that it will stand upright and trim the tips of the leaves with scissors.
2. Place in a pan of boiling, salted water and simmer for 35-40 minutes. Drain well, then leave to cool upside down.
3. Chop the egg and ham. Mix with remaining ingredients.
4. When the artichoke is cold, remove the centre leaves and the hairy "choke". Stuff the centre of the artichoke with the ham and egg mixture. Garnish and serve.

• FRITTATA OF COURGETTES • AND BACON

2 teaspoons oil
100 g (4 oz) small courgettes, sliced
75 g (3 oz) bacon, chopped
1 small onion, finely chopped
salt
freshly ground black pepper
½ teaspoon dried marjoram
2 eggs, beaten
To garnish:
bacon rolls
cress

Preparation time: 5 minutes
Cooking time: 25 minutes
Oven: 180°C, 350°F, Gas Mark 4

1. Heat the oil in a small pan and lightly fry the courgettes, bacon and onion for 2-3 minutes.
2. Transfer to a small ovenproof gratin dish and stir the mixture around a little to grease the dish. Season with salt and pepper and sprinkle with the dried marjoram. **A**
3. Pour the eggs into the dish and cook in a preheated oven for 20 minutes until firm and lightly browned. Garnish and serve at once.

A The courgette and bacon mixture can be prepared 2-3 hours in advance, if covered and chilled.

A frittata is a flat, oven-baked omelette which can be made with a variety of fillings. Small amounts of vegetables can be used in it, particularly leftover cooked vegetables, as well as small quantities of meat such as ham and chicken. Following the basic recipe, try using chicken and sweetcorn or ham and peppers; to make the frittata even more substantial add a small cooked potato.

A globe artichoke is an ideal snack for one person. It also makes an excellent starter for a dinner party. It can be served either stuffed as opposite, or with a vinaigrette dressing or mayonnaise. Alternatively, it may be served hot with melted butter. To eat an artichoke, the leaves should be pulled off one by one, and dipped in the dressing. Only the soft ends of the leaves are eaten. When all the leaves have been pulled off, the inedible choke in the middle of the fleshy base should be scooped out. The tender artichoke base can be eaten with a small spoon.

CLOCKWISE FROM THE TOP: Chicken pilaff with lemon and mint, Frittata of courgettes and bacon, Stuffed globe artichoke

• HOT PRAWN AND CHEESE MUFFINS •

50 g (2 oz) peeled prawns
25 g (1 oz) Cheddar cheese, grated
pinch of cayenne pepper
1 teaspoon grated onion
1 tablespoon mayonnaise
salt
freshly ground black pepper
1 muffin
To garnish:
a few peeled prawns
sprig of dill

Preparation time: 5 minutes
Cooking time: 5 minutes

1. In a bowl, mix together the prawns, cheese, cayenne, grated onion, mayonnaise, salt and pepper.
2. Split the muffin in half and divide the mixture between the 2 halves. Place under a preheated grill and grill until bubbling. Garnish and serve hot.

FROM THE LEFT: Hot prawn and cheese muffins, Sausage, leek and potato gratin, Croissants with creamed mushrooms

• SAUSAGE, LEEK AND POTATO GRATIN •

1 small onion, peeled and chopped
1/2 teaspoon mixed dried herbs
salt
freshly ground black pepper
100 g (4 oz) sausage meat
25 g (1 oz) butter
100 g (4 oz) leeks, washed and thinly sliced
1 medium potato, peeled
To garnish:
2 bay leaves
sprig of rosemary

Preparation time: 10 minutes
Cooking time: 30 minutes
Oven: 190°C, 375°F, Gas Mark 5

1. In a bowl, work the chopped onion, mixed herbs, salt and pepper into the sausage meat. Press the mixture into the bottom of an ovenproof gratin dish.
2. Melt the butter in a pan, add the leeks and salt and pepper. Cook for 3 minutes. Grate the potato into the pan with the leeks and cook for a further 2 minutes. Mix the leeks and potatoes well together, then put on top of the sausage meat.
3. Cook in a preheated oven for 25 minutes. Garnish and serve immediately.

• CROISSANTS WITH CREAMED • MUSHROOMS

2 croissants
25 g (1 oz) butter
100 g (4 oz) mushrooms, peeled and sliced
15 g (½ oz) flour
150 ml (¼ pint) milk
1 tablespoon double or whipping cream
salt
freshly ground black pepper
To garnish:
tomato wedges

Preparation time: 5 minutes
Cooking time: 10 minutes

1. Warm the croissants in a cool oven, while preparing the sauce.
2. Melt the butter in a pan, add the mushrooms and cook for 3 minutes. Add the flour to the pan and cook for 1 minute, then add the milk. Bring to the boil and cook for 3 minutes, stirring all the time, to make a thick smooth sauce, then add the cream, salt and pepper.
3. Cut each warmed croissant in half horizontally and put the bases on a warmed plate. Divide the mushroom sauce between them and replace the tops. Garnish and serve immediately.

• BAKED POTATO STUFFED WITH • SALAMI AND SWEETCORN

1 large baking potato
25 g (1 oz) butter
25 g (1 oz) snack salami, sliced
½ × 200 g (7 oz) can sweetcorn, drained
salt
freshly ground black pepper
15 g (½ oz) Cheddar cheese, grated

Preparation time: 5 minutes
Cooking time: 1 hour
Oven: 230°C, 450°F, Gas Mark 8

1. Scrub and prick the potato, rub with a little of the butter and cook in a preheated oven for about 55 minutes.
2. Remove the potato from the oven, cut in half, scoop out the flesh and put into a bowl. Mash the flesh well with the butter then add the salami, sweetcorn, salt and pepper.
3. Pile the mixture back into the potato cases and sprinkle with the grated cheese. Replace in the oven for about 5 minutes to heat through and brown the cheese.

· PITTA BREAD PIZZAS WITH ·
PEPPERS AND SMOKED HAM

1 pitta bread
1 tablespoon olive oil
1 × 225 g (8 oz) can tomatoes, drained and chopped
½ teaspoon dried oregano
salt
freshly ground black pepper
½ small green pepper, cored, seeded and sliced
½ small red pepper, cored, seeded and sliced
25 g (1 oz) smoked ham, cubed
75 g (3 oz) Mozzarella cheese, grated
To garnish:
tomato wedges
sprig of thyme

Preparation time: 10 minutes
Cooking time: 5 minutes

1. Cut the pitta bread in half horizontally. Place the cooked sides on a baking sheet and brush the uncooked sides with a little olive oil.
2. Put the tomatoes on the bread, spreading them as near to the edge as possible. Sprinkle on the oregano, then season with salt and pepper.
3. Put alternate slices of red and green pepper on top of the tomatoes, then add the smoked ham and grated cheese. Drizzle a little more olive oil over the top of the pizzas.
4. Place under a preheated grill, not too near the element, to make sure everything is heated through, and grill for about 5 minutes. Garnish and serve at once.

· FENNEL BRAISED WITH BACON ·

1 × 100-150 g (4-5 oz) bulb of fennel
15 g (½ oz) butter
2 rashers streaky bacon, rinded and chopped
1 small onion, peeled and chopped
85 ml (3 fl oz) stock
salt
freshly ground black pepper
To garnish:
chopped parsley

Preparation time: 5 minutes
Cooking time: 15 minutes

1. Prepare the fennel by cutting downwards into 8, then trimming a little of the core at the base of each piece.
2. Melt the butter in a pan, add the bacon and onion and cook for 2 minutes. Add the fennel to the pan and stir around to coat with the butter.
3. Add the stock to the pan, season with salt and pepper and bring to the boil. Lower the heat, cover the pan and cook for about 10 minutes until the fennel is cooked through, but still crunchy.
4. Serve sprinkled with the chopped parsley.

· SMOKED MACKEREL PÂTÉ WITH ·
APPLE AND HORSERADISH

✓

1 small dessert apple, peeled and cored
2 teaspoons lemon juice
100 g (4 oz) smoked mackerel, flaked
50 g (2 oz) curd cheese
25 g (1 oz) butter, melted
1 teaspoon creamed horseradish
freshly ground black pepper
To serve:
flat-leaved parsley
French bread or hot toast

Preparation time: 10 minutes

1. Cut 3 slices from the apple, brush with lemon juice and reserve. Grate remaining apple and mix with lemon juice.
2. Put the mackerel, cheese, butter, grated apple and horseradish into a bowl. Mix well, then season with pepper. Ⓐ

3. To serve, put the mixture in a serving dish and garnish with the reserved apple and parsley.

Ⓐ The pâté can be made up to 2 days in advance, if covered and chilled.

• MEXICAN FIRE WITH TORTILLA CHIPS •

2 teaspoons oil
1 small green chilli pepper, cored, seeded and chopped
1 garlic clove, peeled and crushed
1 × 150 ml (5 fl oz) carton soured cream
pinch of dried oregano
1 teaspoon ground cumin
salt
freshly ground black pepper
To serve:
tortilla chips

Preparation time: 5 minutes, plus cooling
Cooking time: 2-3 minutes

1. Heat the oil in a small pan, add the chilli and garlic and cook gently for 2-3 minutes. Leave to cool.
2. Put the soured cream into a bowl and add the oregano, cumin, salt and pepper, then add the cooled chilli, garlic and remaining oil. Mix well. Ⓐ
3. Transfer to a small serving dish and sprinkle with paprika pepper. Serve with tortilla chips.

Ⓐ This dip is best made 2-3 hours in advance to allow the flavours to develop, but can be made 1 day in advance. Keep covered and chilled.

FROM THE LEFT: Pitta bread pizzas with peppers and smoked ham, Smoked mackerel pâté with apple and horseradish, Mexican fire with tortilla chips

• OMELETTE ÎLE DE FRANCE •

25 g (1 oz) butter
15 g (½ oz) plain flour
150 ml (¼ pint) milk
salt
freshly ground black pepper
50 g (2 oz) button mushrooms, sliced
2 eggs, beaten
1 slice cooked ham
25 g (1 oz) Gruyère or Cheddar cheese, grated

Preparation time: 10 minutes
Cooking time: 10-12 minutes

1. Melt half the butter in a small pan, add the flour and cook for 1 minute. Add the milk, salt and pepper, bring to the boil and cook for 2 minutes. Remove half the sauce from the pan, add the mushrooms to the remaining sauce and cook for 1 minute. **A**

2. Melt the remaining butter in a small frying pan. Add the beaten eggs and cook gently over a low heat until the top of the mixture begins to set.

3. Put the slice of ham on top of the eggs, then pour the mushroom sauce on one side of the ham. Fold the omelette.
4. Spread the remaining sauce over the top of the omelette, sprinkle with the grated cheese, then place under a preheated grill until the cheese is bubbling and browned.
5. Serve immediately with a green salad.

Ⓐ The sauce can be made 1 day in advance, if covered and chilled.

• POACHED EGGS FLAMANDE •

175 g (6 oz) Brussels sprouts, peeled
1 medium potato, peeled and diced
salt
25 g (1 oz) butter
1 small onion, peeled and chopped
1 tablespoon milk
freshly ground black pepper
2 eggs
To garnish:
2 rashers streaky bacon, grilled until crisp
chervil leaves

Preparation time: 10 minutes
Cooking time: 20 minutes

1. Put the Brussels sprouts and potato into a pan of lightly salted, boiling water, then simmer until soft. Drain well.
2. Wipe out the pan, melt the butter, then add the onion and cook until softened. Add the Brussels sprouts, potato, milk and pepper. Mash well over the heat until the mixture is creamy. Put into a small gratin dish and keep warm.
3. Meanwhile poach the eggs in simmering salted water for 3 minutes. Drain well then place on top of the Brussels sprouts purée.
4. Chop the bacon into small pieces and sprinkle over the top with the chervil. Serve.

• SCRAMBLED EGGS WITH • SMOKED TROUT

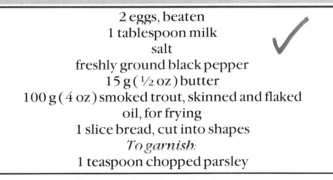

2 eggs, beaten
1 tablespoon milk
salt
freshly ground black pepper
15 g (½ oz) butter
100 g (4 oz) smoked trout, skinned and flaked
oil, for frying
1 slice bread, cut into shapes
To garnish:
1 teaspoon chopped parsley

Preparation time: 5 minutes
Cooking time: 5 minutes

1. Beat together the eggs, milk, salt and pepper.
2. Melt the butter in a pan, add the eggs and cook very slowly, stirring all the time, until the mixture starts to thicken. Add the smoked trout and continue cooking until the eggs are creamy and the trout heated through.
3. While the eggs are cooking, heat the oil in a pan and fry the bread shapes on both sides until brown.
4. Serve with the fried bread and garnished with parsley.

Omelette île de France, Poached eggs Flamande

• SPICED CHICKEN AND •
CAULIFLOWER SALAD

1 × 100 g (4 oz) boned chicken breast, skinned
2 teaspoons oil
½ teaspoon curry powder
½ teaspoon garam masala
½ teaspoon turmeric
salt
freshly ground black pepper
85 ml (3 fl oz) stock
75 g (3 oz) piece cauliflower, cut into tiny florets
2 tablespoons mayonnaise
2 teaspoons mango chutney
½ small green pepper, cored, seeded and diced
½ small red pepper, cored, seeded and diced
25 g (1 oz) salted cashew nuts

Preparation time: 10 minutes, plus cooling
Cooking time: 15 minutes

1. Cut the chicken into small cubes. Heat the oil in a pan and lightly fry the chicken. Add the curry powder, garam masala, turmeric, salt and pepper to the pan and cook for 2 minutes.
2. Add the stock to the pan and bring to the boil. Cover the pan and cook for about 10 minutes.
3. Transfer the chicken and juices to a bowl. Add the cauliflower, mix well and leave to go cold. Ⓐ
4. When cold add the mayonnaise, mango chutney and most of the red and green pepper. Mix well.
5. Place the salad on a small oval serving dish or in a bowl. Arrange the cashew nuts along the centre of the chicken. Mix the remaining red and green peppers together and sprinkle them on each side of the cashew nuts.

Ⓐ The chicken and cauliflower can be prepared up to 1 day in advance, if covered and chilled.

Pitta breads are flat oval breads which originated in the Middle East. White or wholemeal varieties are available. Traditionally, they are filled with kebabs, but the pockets are also ideal for many other snacks, especially for packed lunches and picnics. They can be filled with chunky salads or any variety of sandwich fillings, such as sausages or beef-burgers. If they are cut down one side they can be filled with an omelette and if cut in half horizontally they can be toasted to serve with pâtés. They also make a very quick pizza base (see page 16) – as long as the tomatoes and cheese are retained, the other ingredients can be varied according to what you have available.

• MOROCCAN SALAD MÉCHOUIA •

1 × 90 g (3½ oz) can tuna fish in oil
½ small green pepper, cored, seeded and sliced
1 medium tomato, seeded and cut into chunks
1 teaspoon capers
1 teaspoon lemon juice
1 small garlic clove, peeled and crushed
dash of Tabasco sauce
salt
freshly ground black pepper
1 pitta bread
To garnish:
slice of lemon
sprig of dill

Preparation time: 10 minutes

1. Put the tuna fish and oil into a bowl. Add the green pepper, tomato, capers, lemon juice, garlic, Tabasco, salt and pepper. Mix everything together.
2. Cut the pitta bread in half to make 2 pockets. Fill the pockets with the tuna fish mixture. Garnish with the lemon slice and sprig of dill and serve.

• PAW PAW SALAD WITH GOAT'S • CHEESE AND WALNUTS

1 small paw paw
6 small sprigs watercress
25 g (1 oz) goat's cheese
25 g (1 oz) walnuts, chopped
1 tablespoon oil, walnut if possible
1 teaspoon white wine vinegar
salt
freshly ground black pepper

Preparation time: 5 minutes

1. Cut the paw paw in half, peel and remove the black seeds.
2. Slice the paw paw and arrange the slices in a circle on a flat plate. Place the sprigs of watercress amongst the slices.
3. Crumble the goat's cheese over the top and sprinkle with the walnuts.
4. Mix together the oil, vinegar, salt and pepper and pour over the salad. Ⓐ

Ⓐ The salad can be prepared 3-4 hours in advance, if chilled.

CLOCKWISE FROM THE TOP: Spiced chicken and cauliflower salad, Paw paw salad with goat's cheese and walnuts, Moroccan salad méchouia

MEAT AND POULTRY

• VEAL ESCALOPE WITH TOMATO • CREAM SAUCE AND ALMONDS

1 teaspoon flour
salt
freshly ground black pepper
1 × 100 g (4 oz) veal escalope
15 g (½ oz) butter
1 shallot, peeled and chopped
50 ml (2 fl oz) dry white wine
2 tablespoons single cream
1 tomato, peeled, seeded and cut into strips
1 teaspoon flaked almonds
To garnish:
tomato wedges
sprig of parsley

Preparation time: 5 minutes
Cooking time: 10 minutes

1. Combine flour, salt and pepper and coat the veal with it.
2. Fry the shallot in melted butter for 2 minutes. Add the veal to the pan and cook for 2-3 minutes each side.
3. Add the wine to the pan and boil until reduced to about 1 tablespoonful.
4. Add cream, tomato and almonds and heat gently.
5. Put the veal on to a plate and pour the sauce over. Garnish and serve at once with a salad.

• STEAK AND KIDNEY ROULADE •

2 teaspoons oil
1 small onion, peeled and chopped
1 lamb's kidney, cored and chopped
1 × 150 g (5 oz) thin slice of skirt steak
50 g (2 oz) mushrooms, sliced
½ teaspoon cornflour
85 ml (3 fl oz) beef stock
salt
freshly ground black pepper

Preparation time: 10 minutes, plus cooling
Cooking time: 50 minutes

A thin slice of meat spread with a forcemeat stuffing and then rolled into a sausage shape is often termed a roulade.

1. Heat the oil in a pan and lightly fry the onion and kidney. Remove from the pan, leaving the oil. Cool slightly.
2. Lay out the skirt steak and cover with the onion and kidney mixture. Roll up and secure with fine string or cocktail sticks to prevent the filling from coming out.

3. Fry the roulade in the oil remaining in the pan until brown on all sides. Add the mushrooms to the pan and cook lightly.
4. Mix the cornflour with the beef stock and pour over the roulade. Season with the salt and pepper.
5. Bring to the boil, cover the pan and cook for 45 minutes, turning the roulade occasionally. Remove the string or cocktail sticks before serving.

• BEEF AND SPINACH GRATIN •

175 g (6 oz) lean minced beef
1 small onion, peeled and chopped
1 teaspoon tomato purée
3 tablespoons water
pinch of dried oregano
pinch of dried basil
salt
freshly ground black pepper
225 g (8 oz) spinach, washed and shredded
1 egg yolk
3 tablespoons plain unsweetened yogurt
15 g (½ oz) Cheddar cheese, grated
To garnish:
sprig of oregano
onion rings

Preparation time: 10 minutes
Cooking time: 30 minutes
Oven: 190°C, 375°F, Gas Mark 5

1. Place the minced beef and onion in a non-stick pan and cook until the meat is no longer pink.
2. Add the tomato purée, water, herbs, salt and pepper to the pan and bring to the boil.
3. Add the spinach to the pan and cook for 2-3 minutes until the spinach becomes floppy. Transfer the mixture to an ovenproof dish.
3. Mix together the egg yolk, yogurt and cheese and spread over the beef.
4. Place in a preheated oven and cook for 25 minutes until browned. Garnish and serve immediately.

ABOVE: Beef and spinach gratin; BELOW: Veal escalope with tomato cream sauce and almonds

• BEEF TERIYAKI •

1 tablespoon oil
175 g (6 oz) sirloin steak, cut into thin strips
1 teaspoon grated fresh ginger
1 small onion, peeled and chopped
1 garlic clove, peeled and crushed
1 tablespoon soy sauce
2 tablespoons beef stock
1 teaspoon cornflour
1 teaspoon brown sugar
salt
freshly ground black pepper
spring onion, to garnish

Preparation time: 10 minutes
Cooking time: 10 minutes

1. Heat the oil in a frying pan until very hot. Place the steak in the pan and cook quickly on all sides until brown.
2. Push the steak to one side of the pan, then add the ginger, onion and garlic and cook for 3 minutes.
3. Mix together the soy sauce, stock, cornflour, brown sugar, salt and pepper. Pour into the pan and mix well. Bring to the boil, then reduce the heat and simmer for 3 minutes.
4. Garnish with the spring onion, cut into a tassel, if liked, and serve with mange-tout.

FROM THE LEFT: Beef teriyaki, Fillet steak with shallots and wholegrain mustard

• FILLET STEAK WITH SHALLOTS AND • WHOLEGRAIN MUSTARD

10 g (¼ oz) butter
1 teaspoon oil
2 shallots, peeled and chopped
1 × 100 g (4 oz) fillet steak
1 teaspoon wholegrain mustard
50 ml (2 fl oz) double or whipping cream
salt
freshly ground black pepper
To garnish:
tomato wedges
watercress

Preparation time: 5 minutes
Cooking time: 10 minutes

1. Fry the shallots gently for 2-3 minutes in melted butter and oil, then remove from the pan.
2. Put steak into pan and cook for 2-3 minutes each side.
3. When cooked, push the steak to one side of the pan, return the shallots, then add the mustard, cream, salt and pepper. Bring gently to the boil.
4. Pour sauce over the steak and serve immediately.

• DUTCH PORK CHOP •

½ small dessert apple, peeled, cored and chopped
1 teaspoon sultanas
½ teaspoon cinnamon
salt
freshly ground black pepper
1 × 175 g (6 oz) lean pork chop
2 teaspoons oil
150 ml (5 fl oz) apple juice

Preparation time: 5 minutes
Cooking time: 25 minutes

1. Mix together the apple, sultanas, cinnamon, salt and pepper.
2. Cut a deep pocket horizontally in the pork chop and stuff with the apple mixture; any remaining mixture can be cooked with the chop. Secure the stuffing in the chop with a cocktail stick.
3. Heat the oil in a small frying pan and cook the chop for 1 minute each side to brown.
4. Add the apple juice to the pan. Cover and simmer for 20 minutes, turning the chop once. Remove the lid from the pan, increase the heat and boil until the apple juice is reduced to about 2 tablespoons.
5. Remove the cocktail stick and serve the chop with the sauce poured over.

• PORK KEBAB WITH HONEY • AND ORANGE

grated rind and juice of 1 large orange
1 tablespoon clear honey
2 teaspoons soy sauce
salt
freshly ground black pepper
1 × 225 g (8 oz) spare rib pork chop
¼ teaspoon arrowroot
To garnish:
slices of orange

*Preparation time: 5 minutes, plus cooling
and marinating
Cooking time: 20 minutes*

1. Put the orange rind, juice, honey, soy sauce, salt and pepper in a pan. Bring to the boil and simmer for 2-3 minutes. Strain the sauce into a bowl, reserving the rind. Leave to cool.
2. Cut the pork into cubes, discarding the fat and bone. Add to the sauce and mix well. Leave to marinate for 2-3 hours or overnight, covered and chilled.
3. Thread the cubes of pork on to a kebab skewer, place under a preheated grill and cook for 15 minutes, turning frequently.
4. Strain the marinade into a small pan and mix in the arrowroot, bring to the boil and cook for 2-3 minutes. Put the reserved rind back into the pan.
5. To serve, pour the sauce over the kebab.

• FILLET OF PORK WITH COCONUT • CURRY AND MANGO CHUTNEY

175 g (6 oz) tenderloin of pork
2 teaspoons oil
1 small onion, peeled and finely chopped
1 teaspoon madras curry powder
25 g (1 oz) cream of coconut dissolved in
3 tablespoons boiling water
salt
freshly ground black pepper
2 tablespoons plain unsweetened yogurt
3 teaspoons mango chutney
To garnish:
coriander leaf

*Preparation time: 10 minutes
Cooking time: 20 minutes*

1. Cut the tenderloin into 3 pieces, place between 2 sheets of greaseproof paper or cling film and flatten out slightly with a rolling pin.
2. Heat the oil in a small frying pan and fry the pork for 1 minute on each side. Remove the pork from the pan.
3. Add the onion to the pan, cook for 2 minutes, then add the curry powder and cook for a further minute.

4. Pour in the dissolved cream of coconut and season with salt and pepper. Return the pork to the pan, bring to the boil, cover and simmer for 15 minutes, stirring occasionally. Add the yogurt.
5. Place the pork on a warmed plate, pour the sauce over and top each piece of pork with a teaspoon of mango chutney. Garnish and serve.

FROM THE LEFT: Pork kebab with honey and orange, Fillet of pork with coconut curry and mango chutney, Caribbean ham steak

• CARIBBEAN HAM STEAK •

1 teaspoon oil
1 small onion, peeled and chopped
½ small green pepper, cored, seeded and chopped
½ teaspoon curry powder
85 ml (3 fl oz) pineapple juice, from pineapple chunks
½ teaspoon cornflour
2 teaspoons tomato ketchup
salt
freshly ground black pepper
½ × 225 g (8 oz) can pineapple chunks
1 × 175 g (6 oz) ham steak
To garnish:
tomato wedges
pineapple leaves (optional)

Preparation time: 10 minutes
Cooking time: 12 minutes

1. Heat the oil in a pan, add the onion and cook until softened. Add the green pepper and cook for 2 minutes. Add the curry powder to the pan and cook for 1 minute.
2. Mix together the pineapple juice, cornflour, tomato ketchup, salt and pepper, and add to the pan with the pineapple chunks. Bring to the boil and simmer for a few minutes until the mixture becomes syrupy. Ⓐ
3. Meanwhile place the ham steak under a preheated grill and cook for 5 minutes, turning once.
4. To serve, pour the sauce over the ham steak and garnish with tomato slices and pineapple leaves.

Ⓐ The sauce can be made up to 3 days in advance, if kept in a sealed container in the refrigerator.

If this dish is made using vacuum-packed ham steak, the sauce can be made in a frying pan and the ham steak cooked in the sauce for 5 minutes.

• SAUSAGES WITH LENTILS •

1 teaspoon oil
175 g (6 oz) pork sausages with herbs
1 small onion, chopped
50 g (2 oz) mushrooms, sliced
1 celery stick, sliced
50 g (2 oz) lentils de Puy (page 8), soaked overnight
150 ml (¼ pint) stock
salt
freshly ground black pepper

Preparation time: 10 minutes, plus soaking overnight
Cooking time: 20-25 minutes

1. Heat the oil in a frying pan, add the sausages and cook until browned all over.
2. Push the sausages to the side of the pan, add the onion, mushrooms and celery and cook until softened.
3. Add the drained lentils, stock, salt and pepper to the pan. Bring to the boil, stir well, cover and cook for 15-20 minutes, until the stock has been absorbed and the lentils are tender. Serve hot.

• LAMB CUTLETS WITH FLAGEOLETS • AND HERBES DE PROVENCE

2 × 75 g (3 oz) lamb cutlets
1 teaspoon oil
½ teaspoon herbes de Provence
2 shallots, peeled and chopped
1 garlic clove, peeled and crushed
1 tomato, peeled, seeded and chopped
1 × 120 g (4½ oz) can flageolets, drained
salt
freshly ground black pepper
To garnish:
fresh herbs

Preparation time: 5 minutes
Cooking time: 15 minutes

This dish is best cooked in a frying pan which will fit under the grill.

1. Brush the lamb cutlets with oil and sprinkle with a little herbes de Provence on each side.
2. Place in a pan and grill for about 5 minutes each side.
3. Remove the cutlets from the pan and keep warm. Place the pan on the hob and add the shallots and garlic to the juices remaining in the pan. Cook until softened.
4. Add the tomato, flageolets, salt and pepper to the pan. Mix well and heat through.
5. Transfer the mixture to a warmed plate and top with the lamb cutlets. Garnish and serve.

ABOVE: Noisettes of lamb with cucumber and chive sauce; BELOW: Lamb cutlets with flageolets and herbes de Provence

• NOISETTES OF LAMB WITH • CUCUMBER AND CHIVE SAUCE

1 teaspoon oil
2 × 75 g (3 oz) noisettes of lamb
50 g (2 oz) cucumber, peeled and grated
1 teaspoon flour
50 ml (2 fl oz) dry white wine
50 ml (2 fl oz) stock
salt
freshly ground black pepper
To garnish:
cucumber strips
1 teaspoon chives, chopped

Preparation time: 5 minutes
Cooking time: 15 minutes

1. Heat the oil in a pan and fry the noisettes for 10 minutes, turning once.
2. When the noisettes are cooked, push to one side of the pan then add the cucumber and stir around.
3. Sprinkle in the flour and cook for 1-2 minutes to absorb the liquid.
4. Add the wine, stock, salt and pepper to the pan, bring to the boil and simmer for 2-3 minutes.
5. Serve the noisettes coated with the sauce and sprinkled with the chopped chives and cucumber strips.

This recipe is an excellent partner to all the above dishes.

GLAZED CARROTS

15 g (½ oz) butter
175 g (6 oz) small carrots, peeled
1 teaspoon sugar
salt
freshly ground black pepper
50 ml (2 fl oz) water or stock
1 teaspoon chopped fresh parsley

Preparation time: 5 minutes
Cooking time: 15 minutes

1. Melt the butter in a small saucepan. Add the carrots and stir them around until they are thoroughly coated with the butter.
2. Add the sugar, salt and pepper, and water or stock to the pan. Bring to the boil, cover the pan and simmer gently for 10 minutes, stirring the carrots from time to time.
3. Uncover the pan, raise the heat and cook until all the liquid has evaporated, leaving the carrots with just a buttery glaze. Serve sprinkled with the chopped parsley.

· LAMB CHOP PARCELS WITH ·
APRICOTS AND SESAME SEEDS

2 × 50-75 g (2-3 oz) lamb chops, trimmed of fat
salt
freshly ground black pepper
4 canned unsweetened apricot halves
50 ml (2 fl oz) apricot juice from can
1 teaspoon cornflour
1 teaspoon sesame seeds
To garnish:
flat-leaved parsley
To serve:
long-grain rice, cooked (optional)

Preparation time: 5 minutes
Cooking time: 30 minutes
Oven: 200°C, 400°F, Gas Mark 6

1. Place a large piece of foil on a baking sheet, place the lamb chops on the foil and season with salt and pepper.
2. Put 2 apricot halves on top of each chop.
3. Combine the apricot juice and cornflour and pour over the chops. Fold the foil around the chops to make a well-sealed parcel. Bake in a preheated oven for 30 minutes.
4. Transfer the chops and apricots to a warmed plate, pour the sauce over and sprinkle with the sesame seeds. Garnish with flat-leaved parsley and serve with plain boiled rice, if desired.

• CALVES' LIVER AND BACON • BROCHETTE WITH SAGE

175 g (6 oz) calves' liver in 1 piece
salt
freshly ground black pepper
3 rashers streaky bacon, rinded
To garnish:
6 sage leaves

Preparation time: 5 minutes
Cooking time: 10 minutes

1. Cut the calves' liver into 5 or 6 cubes. Season with salt and pepper.

2. Cut each bacon rasher in half and wrap a piece around each cube of liver.
3. Thread the cubes on to a kebab skewer alternately with the sage leaves.
4. Place the brochette under a preheated hot grill and cook for 10 minutes, turning frequently. Garnish with the sage leaves and serve hot with cubes of fried potatoes, if desired.

• ESCALOPE OF LIVER GREMOLATA •

50 g (2 oz) fresh white breadcrumbs
1 tablespoon chopped fresh parsley
1 teaspoon grated lemon rind
1 small garlic clove, peeled and crushed
salt
freshly ground black pepper
175 g (6 oz) thin slices of lamb's liver
1 tablespoon plain flour
1 egg (size 4), beaten
oil, for frying
To garnish:
lemon wedges
sprig of parsley

Preparation time: 10 minutes, plus chilling
Cooking time: 4-6 minutes

1. Mix together the breadcrumbs, parsley, lemon rind, garlic, salt and pepper.
2. Coat the liver with the flour, dip into the egg, then coat with the breadcrumb mixture. Chill for at least 30 minutes.
3. Heat the oil in a small frying pan and cook the liver for 2-3 minutes each side. Drain on paper towels.
4. Garnish the escalope with the lemon wedges and parsley sprig and serve hot.

FROM THE LEFT: Lamb chop parcels with apricots and sesame seeds, Calves' liver and bacon brochette with sage

• BREAST OF TURKEY WITH LEMON, • ROSEMARY AND SPRING ONION

1 teaspoon flour
salt
freshly ground black pepper
1 × 175 g (6 oz) turkey breast fillet, sliced
15 g (½ oz) butter
2 spring onions, chopped
½ teaspoon dried rosemary
85 ml (3 fl oz) chicken stock
1 teaspoon lemon juice
2 lemon slices
To garnish:
sprig of rosemary

Preparation time: 5 minutes
Cooking time: 10 minutes

1. Combine flour, salt and pepper and coat the turkey slices with it. Melt the butter in a frying pan, add the turkey slices and cook for 2-3 minutes each side.
2. Add the remaining ingredients, bring to the boil and simmer uncovered until the mixture becomes syrupy.
4. Place the turkey on a warmed plate, top with the lemon slices and pour the sauce over the top. Garnish and serve.

• BREAST OF CHICKEN WITH • MUSTARD AND PECAN NUTS

1 × 150 g (5 oz) boned chicken breast, skinned
2 teaspoons French mustard
1 egg (size 4), beaten
15 g (½ oz) fresh white breadcrumbs
15 g (½ oz) pecan nuts, chopped
oil, for frying
15 g (½ oz) flour
120 ml (4 fl oz) milk
salt
freshly ground black pepper
To garnish:
pecan nuts
flat-leaved parsley

Preparation time: 10 minutes, plus chilling
Cooking time: 20 minutes

1. Spread the chicken breast with 1½ teaspoons of the mustard. Dip into the beaten egg.
2. Combine breadcrumbs and pecan nuts and coat chicken breast with this mixture. Chill for at least 30 minutes.
3. Heat the oil in a pan and fry the chicken for 5-7 minutes each side. Remove from the pan and keep warm.
4. Pour off and discard most of the oil, add the flour to the pan and cook for 1 minute. Add the milk, remaining mustard and salt and pepper to the pan. Bring to the boil and simmer for 2 minutes.
5. Strain the sauce and serve with the garnished chicken.

• GRILLED POUSSIN WITH TARRAGON • AND GRAPES

1 × 450 g (1 lb) poussin
1 teaspoon oil
1 teaspoon lemon juice
200 ml (7 fl oz) chicken stock
½ teaspoon dried tarragon
1 tablespoon double or whipping cream
50 g (2 oz) seedless green grapes
salt
freshly ground black pepper
To garnish:
fresh tarragon

Preparation time: 5 minutes
Cooking time: 25 minutes

This is best made in a small meat tin or ovenproof gratin dish that will fit under the grill.

1. Cut the poussin down the backbone and flatten out. Keep the poussin flat by pushing 2 skewers through from leg to leg and wing to wing.
2. Place in the tin or dish, brush with the oil and sprinkle with the lemon juice. Pour the stock around the poussin and add the dried tarragon.
3. Place under a preheated hot grill for about 20 minutes, turning frequently.
4. When cooked, remove the poussin and keep warm. Strain the remaining juices into a small saucepan. (There should be about 3 tablespoons remaining. If there is more, reduce over heat until 3 tablespoons remain.)
5. Add the cream, grapes and salt and pepper to the pan and bring to the boil.
6. To serve, remove the skewers from the poussin, pour the sauce over and garnish with the fresh tarragon.

FROM THE LEFT: Breast of chicken with mustard and pecan nuts, Breast of turkey with lemon, rosemary and spring onion, Grilled poussin with tarragon and grapes

• TANDOORI CHICKEN KEBABS •

1 × 175 g (6 oz) chicken breast fillet, skinned
3 tablespoons plain unsweetened yogurt
2 teaspoons lemon juice
2 teaspoons tandoori spice mix
salt
freshly ground black pepper
1 teaspoon oil

Preparation time: 5 minutes, plus marinating
Cooking time: 10 minutes

1. Cut the chicken breast into cubes. Mix together the yogurt, lemon juice, tandoori spices, salt and pepper.
2. Combine the chicken with the tandoori mixture. Cover and marinate for at least 2-3 hours in the refrigerator.
3. Thread the chicken on to a skewer and brush with oil.
4. Place the kebabs under a preheated grill and cook for 10 minutes, turning frequently.
5. Serve with yellow rice and mango chutney. Garnish with tomato, onion, orange, parsley and cucumber.

• MEXICAN CHICKEN AND • RED BEAN CASSEROLE

1 teaspoon oil
175 g (6 oz) boneless chicken thighs, cut into chunks
1 small onion, chopped
1 small garlic clove, peeled and crushed
1/4 teaspoon chilli powder
120 ml (4 fl oz) chicken stock
2 teaspoons tomato purée
1/2 teaspoon dried oregano
salt
freshly ground black pepper
1/2 × 213 g (7 1/2 oz) can red kidney beans
To garnish:
sliced red pepper
oregano sprig

Preparation time: 5 minutes
Cooking time: 30 minutes

1. Heat the oil in a pan, add the chicken, onion and garlic and cook until the chicken is lightly browned. Add the chilli powder to the pan and cook for 1 minute.
2. Add the stock, tomato purée, oregano and salt and pepper to the pan. Bring to the boil, cover the pan and simmer for 20 minutes, stirring occasionally.
3. Add the kidney beans to the pan, bring back to the boil and simmer for a further 5 minutes. Serve at once.

FROM THE LEFT: Tandoori chicken kebabs, Mexican chicken and red bean casserole

FISH DISHES

✓ • CRAB AND PINK GRAPEFRUIT SALAD •

4 or 5 small lettuce leaves
50-75 g (2-3 oz) white crab meat
1 tablespoon oil
1 teaspoon lemon juice
1 celery stick, sliced
50 g (2 oz) black grapes, halved and seeded
salt
freshly ground black pepper
1 pink grapefruit, cut into segments
1 teaspoon flaked almonds

Preparation time: 10 minutes

1. Place the lettuce leaves on one side of a small plate.
2. Mix together the crab, oil, lemon juice, celery and black grapes and season with salt and pepper. Pile the mixture on the plate, opposite the lettuce leaves.
3. Arrange the grapefruit segments along the centre of the plate, in between the lettuce and the crab.
4. Sprinkle the flaked almonds over the crab.

✓ • FRESH PASTA WITH CRAB AND • COURGETTES

100 g (4 oz) courgettes, ends removed
25 g (1 oz) butter
1 garlic clove, peeled and crushed
100 g (4 oz) fresh pasta, such as green and white linguine
75 g (3 oz) white crab meat
1 teaspoon lemon juice
salt
freshly ground black pepper
To garnish:
lemon wedges
1 teaspoon chopped parsley or a sprig

Preparation time: 10 minutes
Cooking time: 10 minutes

1. Cut the courgettes into slices lengthways, then again lengthways to make thin strips.
2. Melt the butter in a pan, add the garlic and cook for 2 minutes. Add the courgettes to the pan and cook for a further 3 minutes, stirring frequently.
3. While the courgettes are cooking, bring a pan of salted water to the boil and cook the pasta for 3 minutes. Drain well.
4. Add the pasta to the pan with the courgettes, then add the crab, lemon juice, salt and pepper. Stir well and reheat gently to make sure the crab is heated through.

5. Transfer the mixture to a warmed plate. Garnish with the lemon wedges and chopped parsley or parsley sprig.

✓ • PRAWN AND PASTA SALAD •

75 g (3 oz) pasta bows
1 garlic clove, peeled and crushed
1 tablespoon olive oil
1 tablespoon lemon juice
50 g (2 oz) peeled prawns
1 tomato, peeled, seeded and cut into strips
1 celery stick, sliced
6 stuffed olives, sliced
salt
freshly ground black pepper
To garnish:
2 whole prawns
sprig of dill

Preparation time: 10 minutes, plus cooling
Cooking time: 10 minutes

1. Bring a pan of salted water to the boil and cook the pasta for 10 minutes. Drain well and leave until cold. Ⓐ
2. Mix together the garlic, olive oil and lemon juice. Add the cooled pasta, prawns, tomatoes, celery, olives, salt and pepper. Place on a dish and garnish with whole prawns and sprig of dill.

Ⓐ The pasta can be cooked up to 2 days in advance if kept covered and chilled.

CLOCKWISE FROM THE TOP: Crab and pink grapefruit salad, Prawn and pasta salad, Fresh pasta with crab and courgettes

• SCAMPI PROVENÇALE •

1 tablespoon olive oil
1 small onion, peeled and chopped
1 garlic clove, peeled and crushed
50 ml (2 fl oz) dry white wine
1½ tomatoes
1 teaspoon tomato purée
3 tablespoons water
½ bunch fresh parsley
¼ teaspoon dried thyme
salt
freshly ground black pepper
100 g (4 oz) scampi, peeled
sprig of parsley, to garnish

Preparation time: 10 minutes
Cooking time: 10 minutes

1. Heat the oil in a pan and cook the onion and garlic until softened. Add the wine to the pan, bring to the boil, then simmer until reduced slightly.
2. Reserve a slice of tomato for garnishing, and peel, seed and chop the remainder. Add the chopped tomatoes, tomato purée, water, 1 teaspoon of chopped parsley and thyme to the pan. Cook for 5 minutes. Season with salt and pepper.
3. Add the scampi to the pan and heat through.
4. Garnish with tomato slice and a sprig of parsley and serve with boiled rice.

• BAKED MARINATED COD • ✓

1 tablespoon olive oil
1 small garlic clove, peeled and crushed
¼ teaspoon chilli powder
1 teaspoon lemon juice
½ teaspoon dried mint
salt
freshly ground black pepper
175 g (6 oz) middle cut cod fillet, skinned
25 g (1 oz) fresh white breadcrumbs
15 g (½ oz) Parmesan cheese, grated
To garnish:
2 wedges of lemon
1 sprig fresh mint

Preparation time: 5 minutes, plus marinating
Cooking time: 20 minutes
Oven: 190°C, 375°F, Gas Mark 5

1. Mix together the olive oil, garlic, chilli powder, lemon juice, dried mint, salt and pepper. Place the cod in this mixture, cover and chill for 2-3 hours or overnight, turning frequently.
2. Remove the cod from the marinade and place in a small ovenproof gratin dish with just enough of the marinade to keep it moist.
3. Mix together the breadcrumbs and Parmesan cheese and press on to the top of the cod. Drizzle a teaspoonful of the marinade over the top and cook in a preheated oven for 20 minutes.
4. Serve garnished with wedges of lemon and a sprig of fresh mint.

• WHOLE PLAICE WITH ORANGE • ✓

1 × 225 g (8 oz) whole plaice
1 teaspoon seasoned flour
25 g (1 oz) butter
2 slices orange
1 tablespoon orange juice
1 teaspoon chopped fresh parsley
salt
freshly ground black pepper

Preparation time: 5 minutes
Cooking time: 12 minutes

1. Coat the fish with the seasoned flour.
2. Melt the butter in a small frying pan and cook the plaice gently for about 10 minutes, turning once.
3. Transfer the fish to a warmed plate, top with the orange slices and keep warm.
4. Add the orange juice, parsley, salt and pepper to the pan and bring to the boil, stirring well.
5. Pour the sauce over the fish and serve at once.

FROM THE LEFT: Scampi Provençale, Whole plaice with orange

• LEMON SOLE JULIENNE •

1 carrot, peeled and cut into thin sticks
25 g (1 oz) fine French beans, topped and tailed
1 courgette, topped and tailed and cut into thin sticks
15 g (½ oz) butter
175 g (6 oz) lemon sole fillets, cut into diagonal strips
1 teaspoon lemon juice
salt
freshly ground black pepper
1 tablespoon double or whipping cream
sprig of dill, to garnish

Preparation time: 10 minutes
Cooking time: 10-15 minutes

1. Bring a pan of salted water to the boil, add the carrot and French beans and cook for 3 minutes. Add the courgette and cook for a further 2 minutes. Drain well.
2. Melt the butter in a small pan, add the strips of sole and cook quickly for 2-3 minutes, stirring all the time.
3. Add the vegetables, lemon juice, salt and pepper to the pan, mix well and cook until heated through. Add the cream to the pan and reheat gently without boiling.
4. Garnish with lemon slices, if desired, and dill.

• KIPPER RAREBIT •

1 × 75-100 g (3-4 oz) kipper fillet
150 ml (¼ pint) milk
15 g (½ oz) butter
15 g (½ oz) flour
freshly ground black pepper
1 slice hot buttered toast
15 g (½ oz) Cheddar cheese, grated

Preparation time: 10 minutes, plus standing
Cooking time: 15 minutes

1. Place the kipper fillet in a small pan with the milk and slowly bring to the boil. Remove from the heat and leave to stand for 5 minutes.
2. Remove the kipper from the milk, reserving the milk. Skin and flake the kipper.
3. Melt the butter in a small pan, add the flour and cook for 2-3 minutes. Add the milk, bring to the boil and simmer for 2-3 minutes. Add the flaked fish and black pepper.
4. Place the toast on a heatproof plate. Pour the fish mixture over the toast and sprinkle with the grated cheese. Place under a preheated grill and cook until the cheese is brown and bubbling.

• SMOKED HADDOCK AND RICE LAYER •

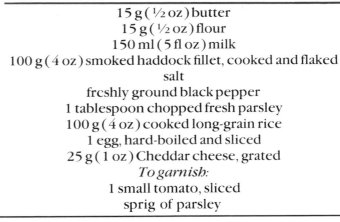

15 g (½ oz) butter
15 g (½ oz) flour
150 ml (5 fl oz) milk
100 g (4 oz) smoked haddock fillet, cooked and flaked
salt
freshly ground black pepper
1 tablespoon chopped fresh parsley
100 g (4 oz) cooked long-grain rice
1 egg, hard-boiled and sliced
25 g (1 oz) Cheddar cheese, grated
To garnish:
1 small tomato, sliced
sprig of parsley

Preparation time: 10 minutes
Cooking time: 30 minutes
Oven: 180°C, 350°F, Gas Mark 4

1. Melt the butter in a small saucepan, add the flour and cook for 1 minute. Add the milk and cook for a further 2 minutes. Add the smoked haddock to the sauce and season with salt and pepper.
2. Mix the parsley with the rice. Place half the rice, half the egg and half the smoked haddock in a small straight-sided dish, such as a soufflé dish. Repeat the layers.
3. Sprinkle the grated cheese over the top. Place the dish in a preheated oven and cook for 20-25 minutes.
4. Serve garnished with the sliced tomato and sprig of parsley.

As a variation to the above recipe you can make some delicious savoury fish cakes by using the same basic ingredients. Omitting the hard-boiled egg and cheese, mix the fish into the sauce, rice and parsley. Chill the mixture, then shape it into 2 flat cakes. Dip them in beaten egg, then in 25 g (1 oz) fresh white breadcrumbs. Fry in hot oil for 3-4 minutes on each side. Drain the fish cakes well on paper towels.

TOP: Smoked haddock and rice layer; BOTTOM: Lemon sole julienne

√ • BAKED STUFFED MACKEREL •

15 g (½ oz) butter
1 small onion, finely chopped
½ small cooking apple, peeled, cored and chopped
25 g (1 oz) fresh white breadcrumbs
1 teaspoon grated lemon rind
salt
freshly ground black pepper
1 mackerel, cleaned and boned
3 tablespoons water
To garnish:
slices of lemon
sprig of dill

Preparation time: 10 minutes
Cooking time: 25 minutes
Oven: 180°C, 350°F, Gas Mark 4

1. Melt the butter in a small pan, add the onion and cook until soft. Add the apple, breadcrumbs, lemon rind, salt and pepper and mix well.
2. Open out the mackerel until it is flat. Place the stuffing in the centre and roll up the fish. Secure the stuffing with wooden cocktail sticks. Ⓐ
3. Place the fish in a small ovenproof dish and pour the water over. Cover the dish with foil and cook in a pre-heated oven for 20 minutes. Remove the cocktail sticks, garnish and serve.

FROM THE LEFT: Baked stuffed mackerel, Haddock steamed in lettuce leaves

Ⓐ If the filling is allowed to go cold before the mackerel is stuffed, the fish can be prepared 2-3 hours in advance. Keep covered and chilled.

• TROUT WITH CUCUMBER • ✔

1 × 225 g (8 oz) trout, skinned and filleted
85 ml (3 fl oz) water
1 teaspoon lemon juice
15 g (½ oz) butter
75 g (3 oz) cucumber, peeled and diced
1 teaspoon cornflour
50 ml (2 fl oz) milk
salt
freshly ground black pepper
To garnish:
sprigs of fresh dill

Preparation time: 5 minutes
Cooking time: 20 minutes
Oven: 180°C, 350°F, Gas Mark 4

1. Place the trout fillets in a baking dish and cover with the water and lemon juice. Cover the dish, place in a pre-heated oven and cook for 15 minutes.
2. Meanwhile, melt the butter in a small pan, add the cucumber and cook for 3 minutes.
3. When the fish is cooked, strain off the liquid and keep warm. Add the cornflour to the cucumber in the pan and mix well. Add the fish liquor, milk, salt and pepper, bring to the boil and cook for 2 minutes.
4. Pour the juices over the fish and garnish with the dill.

• HADDOCK STEAMED IN LETTUCE • ✔ LEAVES

12 lettuce leaves
175 g (6 oz) haddock fillet
salt
freshly ground black pepper
To garnish:
lemon slices
chopped spring onions

Preparation time: 10 minutes
Cooking time: 15-20 minutes

1. Blanch the lettuce leaves by pouring boiling water over them. Drain well, then pat dry with paper towels. Arrange the lettuce leaves in 4 piles, each containing 3 leaves.
2. Cut the haddock into 4 pieces. Place a piece of fish in the centre of each lettuce leaf, season with salt and pepper then wrap the fish in the lettuce to form a parcel. Ⓐ
3. Put the parcels seam-side down into a steamer (if possible a bamboo Chinese steamer). Place the steamer over a pan of simmering water and simmer for about 15 minutes. Garnish and serve immediately.

Ⓐ The parcels can be prepared 2-3 hours in advance, if covered and chilled.

· SKEWERED SARDINES ·

4-6 fresh sardines, cleaned and scaled
1 teaspoon oil
salt
freshly ground black pepper
To serve:
lemon wedges

Preparation time: 5 minutes
Cooking time: 10 minutes

1. Thread the sardines on to a kebab skewer, brush with the oil and season with the salt and pepper.
2. Place under a preheated grill and cook for about 10 minutes, turning frequently.
3. Serve with the lemon wedges.

FROM THE LEFT: Skewered sardines, Herring with oatmeal and almonds, Devilled whiting

· HERRING WITH OATMEAL AND · ALMONDS

1 herring, cleaned, boned, scaled and cut in half
25 g (1 oz) medium oatmeal
25 g (1 oz) blanched almonds, finely chopped
salt
freshly ground black pepper
1 tablespoon milk
1 tablespoon oil
To garnish:
lemon slice
sprig of parsley

Preparation time: 10 minutes
Cooking time: 10 minutes

1. Mix together the oatmeal, almonds, salt and pepper.
2. Dip the herring fillets into the milk, then coat with the oatmeal mixture, pressing it well on to the fish.
3. Heat the oil in a frying pan and cook the herrings for 10

minutes, turning once. Drain well on paper towels.
4. To serve, garnish the herring with the lemon slice and parsley sprig.

• DEVILLED WHITING • ✓

15 g (½ oz) butter
2 whiting fillets, approximately 75 g (3 oz) each
1 tablespoon chutney
1 teaspoon lemon juice
1 teaspoon brown sugar
pinch of mustard powder
pinch of curry powder
salt
freshly ground black pepper
25 g (1 oz) fresh white breadcrumbs
To garnish:
quartered lemon slices
coriander sprig

Preparation time: 10 minutes
Cooking time: 15 minutes
Oven: 200°C, 400°F, Gas Mark 6

1. Use some of the butter to grease a small ovenproof dish thoroughly. Place the fish fillets in the dish.
2. Mix together the chutney, lemon juice, sugar, mustard, curry powder, salt and pepper.
3. Spread half of the mixture over each fish fillet.
4. Sprinkle the fish with the breadcrumbs and dot with the remaining butter.
5. Place in a preheated oven, and cook for 15 minutes.

· MONKFISH WITH HERBS · ✓

2 tablespoons olive oil
2 teaspoons lemon juice
½ teaspoon dried mixed herbs
½ teaspoon dried dill
salt
freshly ground black pepper
175 g (6 oz) monkfish
To garnish:
1 tablespoon chopped fresh parsley or dill

Preparation time: 5 minutes, plus marinating
Cooking time: 10 minutes

1. Mix together the olive oil, lemon juice, herbs, dill, salt and pepper. Place the monkfish in a shallow dish and pour the marinade over. Leave to marinate for at least 1 hour, turning the fish occasionally. A
2. Remove the fish from the marinade and reserve the marinade.
3. Place the fish under a preheated grill and cook for about 10 minutes, turning once and basting occasionally with the reserved marinade.
4. Transfer the fish to a warmed plate and sprinkle with the chopped parsley or dill.

A The fish needs to be marinated for at least 1 hour but can be prepared up to 12 hours in advance, if kept covered and chilled.

· BRAISED HALIBUT CHINESE-STYLE ·

1 tablespoon oil
175 g (6 oz) halibut fillet, cut into chunks
2 slices root ginger, peeled and cut into strips
1 spring onion, cut into strips
2 tablespoons stock
2 teaspoons dry sherry
2 teaspoons soy sauce
¼ teaspoon cornflour
salt
freshly ground black pepper
To garnish:
spring onions
tomato wedges

Preparation time: 10 minutes
Cooking time: 10 minutes

1. Heat the oil in a small frying pan and fry the halibut quickly on all sides until lightly browned. Add the ginger and spring onion to the pan and cook for a further minute.
2. Mix together the stock, sherry, soy sauce, cornflour, salt and pepper and pour over the fish. Bring to the boil, then simmer for 5 minutes, stirring frequently. Garnish and serve immediately.

· SKATE WITH CAPERS AND GHERKINS ·

25 g (1 oz) unsalted butter
225 g (8 oz) skate
1 teaspoon white wine vinegar
1 teaspoon capers, finely chopped
1 teaspoon finely chopped gherkin
salt
freshly ground black pepper
To garnish:
gherkin fan

Preparation time: 5 minutes
Cooking time: 12 minutes

1. Melt the butter in a small frying pan and cook the skate for about 10 minutes, turning once.
2. Remove the fish from the pan and keep warm.
3. Add the vinegar, capers and gherkin to the butter remaining in the pan. Season with salt and pepper and bring to the boil.
4. Pour the sauce over the fish.
5. Garnish and serve immediately.

FROM THE LEFT: Braised halibut Chinese-style, Skate with capers and gherkins

• SALMON WITH WATERCRESS SAUCE •

1 × 175 g (6 oz) salmon steak, skinned
salt
freshly ground black pepper
50 ml (2 fl oz) dry white wine or dry white vermouth
50 ml (2 fl oz) water
1 teaspoon butter, melted
1 teaspoon flour
1 tablespoon double or whipping cream
6 large sprigs watercress, finely chopped
To garnish:
sprig of watercress

Preparation time: 5 minutes
Cooking time: 20 minutes
Oven: 180°C, 350°F, Gas Mark 4

If you have a blender or food processor the whole sprigs of watercress and the rest of the sauce ingredients can be blended for a few seconds, then brought to the boil in a small saucepan and simmered for 2-3 minutes.

1. Place the salmon in a small ovenproof dish, season with salt and pepper and pour over the wine or vermouth and water. Cover with foil, place in a preheated oven and cook for 15 minutes.
2. When the salmon is cooked, strain off the juices into a small saucepan and keep the salmon warm.
3. Mix together the butter and flour and add a little at a time to the liquid in the pan, whisking constantly to make a smooth sauce.
4. Add the cream and watercress to the pan and heat gently.
5. Pour the sauce on to a plate, place the salmon on top and garnish with the sprig of watercress.

This salmon dish is perfect for a very special summer dinner party. For 4 people, buy 2 tail-end pieces of fresh salmon each weighing about 400 g (14 oz) and ask the fishmonger to bone and skin them to make 4 even-sized fillets. Cook the fish as above; the sauce ingredients need only be multiplied by three. Serve the salmon with small new potatoes, and either a green vegetable such as broccoli or French beans, or a mixed salad. Many large supermarkets now sell ready-prepared salads of different lettuce leaves such as curly endive and red-leaved radiccio lettuce. Such salads need only to be tossed in a bowl with a well-flavoured vinaigrette dressing or, better still, some nut oil, with a little of the appropriate nuts chopped and sprinkled over the top. Although nut oils like walnut and hazelnut oil are expensive to buy, a little goes a long way and the oils will keep well in a refrigerator after opening.

TOP: Salmon with watercress sauce; BOTTOM: Red mullet Niçoise en papillote

• RED MULLET NIÇOISE EN PAPILLOTE •

2 teaspoons olive oil
1 small onion, peeled and chopped
1 small garlic clove, peeled and crushed
2 small tomatoes, peeled, seeded and chopped
4 black olives, stoned and chopped
salt
freshly ground black pepper
1 red mullet, gutted and boned
oil, for greasing
1 teaspoon lemon juice

Preparation time: 10 minutes
Cooking time: 20-25 minutes
Oven: 180°C, 350°F, Gas Mark 4

1. Heat the oil in a pan, add the onion and garlic and cook for 1-2 minutes. Add the tomatoes, olives, salt and pepper and stir until coated in oil. Cool, then stuff the mullet with the mixture.
2. Cut two circles of greaseproof paper about 30 cm (12 inches) in diameter, put one on top of the other and lightly grease the top layer. Fold the paper in half and place the fish in the fold. Sprinkle the fish with the lemon juice, then fold and seal the greaseproof paper all around by twisting, rolling or folding the edges to make a parcel. A
3. Place on a baking sheet and cook in a preheated oven for 15-20 minutes. Slit the paper parcel, remove the fish and serve immediately.

A The fish can be prepared 2-3 hours in advance if kept in the refrigerator.

The "en papillote" method of cooking fish is a very good one because it ensures that all the flavours are kept in the paper parcels. Although any fish can be cooked by this method, it is particularly good for small whole fish such as the red mullet above, or for stuffed mackerel and trout. Always make sure that the paper parcel is well sealed so that none of the juices leak out.

WHOLESOME AND HEALTHY

✓ • WHOLEWHEAT PASTA WITH • BROCCOLI AND BLUE CHEESE

75 g (3 oz) wholewheat pasta shells
100 g (4 oz) broccoli, cut into small florets
50 g (2 oz) blue cheese
25 g (1 oz) butter
50 ml (2 fl oz) double or whipping cream
salt
freshly ground black pepper

Preparation time: 5 minutes
Cooking time: 10 minutes

1. Bring a pan of salted water to the boil, add the pasta and cook for 5 minutes. Add the broccoli to the pan and cook for a further 3 minutes. Drain well and remove the pasta and broccoli from the pan.
2. Put the pan back on the heat and add the blue cheese, butter and cream to the pan. Heat gently, stirring all the time to make a smooth sauce. Taste and adjust the seasoning as blue cheese can sometimes be quite salty.
3. Return the pasta and broccoli to the pan . Toss to mix thoroughly with the sauce and heat gently. Serve on a warmed plate.

• FRIED MOZZARELLA AND TOMATO • SANDWICH

4 slices white bread
75 g (3 oz) Mozzarella cheese, sliced
1 medium tomato, sliced
1 egg (size 4), beaten
1 tablespoon milk
½ teaspoon dried basil
salt
freshly ground black pepper
oil, for frying
To garnish:
dried basil

Preparation time: 10 minutes
Cooking time: 3-4 minutes

1. Remove the crusts from the bread and cut each slice into circles. Make 2 sandwiches with the Mozzarella and sliced tomato. Pinch the edges of the bread together to seal.
2. Mix together the egg, milk, dried basil, salt and pepper.
3. Dip both sides of the sandwiches in the egg mixture.
4. Heat the oil in a small frying pan and fry the sandwiches on both sides until golden brown. Garnish with the basil and serve at once.

• BAKED ARTICHOKE BASES STUFFED • WITH MUSHROOMS AND SPINACH

25 g (1 oz) butter
50 g (2 oz) mushrooms, peeled and chopped
1 small onion, peeled and chopped
225 g (8 oz) spinach, washed and shredded
salt
freshly ground black pepper
1 × 300 g (11 oz) can artichoke bases
25 g (1 oz) Cheddar cheese, grated

Preparation time: 10 minutes
Cooking time: 25-30 minutes
Oven: 180°C, 350°F, Gas Mark 4

1. Melt the butter in a pan, add the mushrooms and onions and cook for 3 minutes. Add the spinach to the pan, cover and cook for a further 3 minutes. Uncover the pan, increase the heat and cook until all the liquid has evaporated. Season with salt and pepper.
2. Put the artichoke bases in a small ovenproof gratin dish. Divide the mushroom and spinach mixture between the artichoke bases, spreading any remaining mixture over the top.
3. Sprinkle a little grated cheese over each one. Ⓐ Ⓕ
4. Place in a preheated oven and cook for 20-25 minutes. Serve at once.

Ⓐ The dish can be prepared up to 1 day in advance, if kept covered and chilled.
Ⓕ Freeze for up to 3 months. Defrost overnight in a refrigerator or for 4-6 hours at room temperature.

TOP: Wholewheat pasta with broccoli and blue cheese;
BOTTOM: Fried Mozzarella and tomato sandwich

• COTTAGE CHEESE, SPRING ONION • AND CHIVE FRITTERS

25 g (1 oz) butter
1 small bunch spring onions, chopped
100 g (4 oz) carton cottage cheese with chives
2 tablespoons plain flour
salt
freshly ground black pepper
1 egg, separated
oil, for frying

Preparation time: 10 minutes
Cooking time: 6-7 minutes

1. Melt the butter in a small pan and lightly fry the spring onions.
2. Transfer the onions to a bowl, add the cottage cheese, flour, salt, pepper and egg yolk and mix well. Ⓐ
3. Whisk the egg white until stiff and fold into the cottage cheese mixture.
4. Heat the oil in a frying pan and drop tablespoons of the mixture into the pan. Cook for 2 minutes then turn the fritters over and cook for a further 2 minutes. Drain on paper towels before serving.

Ⓐ The cottage cheese mixture can be prepared 2-3 hours in advance, if covered and chilled.

• FLAMENCO EGGS •

2 teaspoons olive oil
1 small onion, sliced
1 small red pepper, cored, seeded and sliced
1 small garlic clove, peeled and crushed
2 tomatoes, peeled, seeded and chopped
6 stuffed olives, sliced
salt
freshly ground black pepper
2 eggs
To garnish:
flat-leaved parsley

Preparation time: 10 minutes
Cooking time: 10-12 minutes
Oven: 160°C, 325°F, Gas Mark 3

1. Heat the oil in a pan, add the onion, red pepper and garlic and cook until softened. Add the tomatoes, olives, salt and pepper and transfer the mixture to a small oven-proof gratin dish. Ⓐ
2. Make 2 depressions in the vegetables and break an egg into each one.
3. Place in a preheated oven for 5-7 minutes, depending on how you like your eggs cooked. Garnish and serve hot.

Ⓐ The vegetable mixture can be prepared a few hours in advance, if covered and chilled.

• BLUE CHEESE MOUSSE WITH • FRUITS VINAIGRETTES

40 g (1½ oz) creamy blue cheese, grated
2 tablespoons plain unsweetened yogurt
1 tablespoon mayonnaise
1 egg, separated
salt
freshly ground black pepper
2 teaspoons powdered gelatine, dissolved in
2 tablespoons water
oil, for greasing
To garnish:
1 small pear, peeled and sliced
1 small kiwi fruit, peeled and sliced
50 g (2 oz) raspberries
1 tablespoon vinaigrette dressing (below)
sprig of mint

Preparation time: 15 minutes, plus setting

1. Put the cheese, yogurt, mayonnaise and egg yolk into a bowl and mix well. Add salt and pepper and the dissolved gelatine.
2. Whisk the egg white until stiff then fold lightly into the cheese mixture. Pour into an oiled 300 ml (½ pint) mould, preferably a ring mould, and leave to set in the refrigerator.
3. Meanwhile mix the fruit with the vinaigrette dressing.
4. When the mousse is set, unmould and fill the centre with the fruit, or place around the edge.
5. Garnish with a sprig of fresh mint.

VINAIGRETTE DRESSING

6 tablespoons oil
2 tablespoons white wine vinegar
1 teaspoon caster sugar
salt
freshly ground black pepper

Preparation time: 5 minutes

1. Put all the ingredients into a small screw-top jar and shake well. Keep refrigerated and use as required.
This is a standard recipe for vinaigrette, but other ingredients can be added to the basic preparation. Try experimenting with crushed garlic, French mustard or chopped fresh herbs.

FROM THE LEFT: Flamenco eggs, Blue cheese mousse with fruits vinaigrettes

• PASTA TWISTS WITH FRESH • CORIANDER AND WALNUT SAUCE

100 g (4 oz) pasta twists
salt
1 tablespoon olive oil
50 ml (2 fl oz) double or whipping cream
25 g (1 oz) Cheddar cheese, finely grated
25 g (1 oz) walnuts, finely chopped
25 g (1 oz) fresh coriander, finely chopped
salt
freshly ground black pepper
To garnish:
sprig of coriander

Preparation time: 10 minutes
Cooking time: 15 minutes

1. Bring a pan of salted water to the boil, add the pasta and cook for 15 minutes. Drain well.
2. While the pasta is cooking, make the sauce. Place the olive oil and cream in a bowl and add the cheese, walnuts, coriander, salt and black pepper. Mix well together. ▲
3. Place the pasta on a hot dish, pour the sauce on top and mix together. Garnish with the fresh coriander.

▲ The sauce will keep for 1-2 days in a covered container in the refrigerator.

• PERSIAN RICE SALAD •

1 tablespoon olive oil
75 g (3 oz) long-grain rice
½ teaspoon ground cinnamon
½ teaspoon ground allspice
1 × 225 g (8 oz) can apricot halves in syrup, halved
1 tablespoon vinaigrette dressing (page 53)
salt
freshly ground black pepper
50 g (2 oz) dates, stoned and halved
2 teaspoons pine nuts, toasted
To garnish:
sprig of mint

Preparation time: 5 minutes, plus cooling
Cooking time: 25 minutes

1. Heat the oil in a pan and add the rice, cinnamon and allspice. Stir until the rice is coated with the oil and spices.
2. Drain the syrup from the apricots and make up to 250 ml (8 fl oz) with the water. Add to the rice, bring to the boil, cover the pan and simmer for 20 minutes until all the liquid has been absorbed and the rice is tender.
3. While the rice is still hot, stir in the vinaigrette dressing and season with salt and pepper. Ⓐ
4. Leave the rice until completely cold, then add the apricots and dates.
5. Pile on to a serving dish and sprinkle with the toasted pine nuts. Garnish and serve.

Ⓐ The rice can be cooked 1 day in advance, if kept covered and chilled.

The Persian rice salad can also be served as an accompaniment to cold meats; it is particularly good with cold lamb. If the vinaigrette dressing is omitted, it makes a delicious stuffing for a small leg or a shoulder of lamb to serve at a dinner party. For 4 people ask your butcher to bone a small leg or shoulder of lamb. You will need about 1 kg (2 lb) boned weight of lamb. Fill the cavity with the fruit and rice mixture, then tie the joint up neatly with string. Roast in a preheated oven, 180°C, 350°F, Gas Mark 4 for 1½-1¾ hours. Remove the string before serving.

FROM THE LEFT: Pasta twists with fresh coriander and walnut sauce, Persian rice salad

• PARSNIP AND CASHEW NUT • PATTIES WITH CUMIN

225 g (8 oz) parsnips, peeled and diced
salt
25 g (1 oz) butter
1 small onion, peeled and chopped
25 g (1 oz) unsalted cashew nuts, roughly chopped
1 teaspoon ground cumin
freshly ground black pepper
1 tablespoon flour
1 egg (size 4), beaten
50 g (2 oz) wholewheat breadcrumbs
oil, for frying
To garnish:
cos lettuce
radiccio
sprig of parsley

Preparation time: 10 minutes, plus cooling
Cooking time: 30 minutes

1. Cook the parsnips in boiling salted water until very soft, about 15 minutes. Drain, then mash well.
2. Wipe out the pan, then melt the butter. Add the onion and cashew nuts and cook for 2 minutes. Add the cumin to the pan and cook for 1 minute.
3. Return the parsnip purée to the pan and mix well. Season with salt and pepper.
4. Leave the mixture to go cold, then using floured hands shape the mixture into 4 patties. Dip the patties into the beaten egg, then coat with the breadcrumbs.
5. Heat the oil in a pan and cook the patties for 3-4 minutes on each side. Drain on paper towels, garnish and serve.

FROM THE LEFT: Parsnip and cashew nut patties with cumin, Courgette soufflé stuffed tomatoes

• COURGETTE SOUFFLÉ STUFFED • TOMATOES ✓

15 g (½ oz) butter
1 small onion, peeled and finely chopped
1 small courgette, 50-75 g (2-3 oz), topped, tailed
and grated
3 teaspoons flour
3 tablespoons milk
salt
freshly ground black pepper
25 g (1 oz) Gruyère cheese, grated
1 egg (size 4), separated
2 large tomatoes, each 150-175 g (5-6 oz)
To garnish:
courgette slices

Preparation time: 10 minutes
Cooking time: 30-35 minutes
Oven: 190°C, 375°F, Gas Mark 5

1. Melt the butter in a pan, add the onion and courgettes and cook for 2 minutes. Add the flour and cook for a further minute.
2. Add the milk and bring to the boil, stirring all the time. Season, then cook for 2 minutes to make a thick sauce.
3. Remove the pan from the heat, then add most of the cheese and the egg yolk. Stir to mix.
4. Whisk the egg white until stiff, then lightly fold into the courgette mixture.
5. Cut a slice from the top of each tomato, scoop out and discard the seeds. Divide the courgette mixture between the tomatoes and sprinkle with the remaining cheese.
6. Place the tomatoes in a small ovenproof dish and bake in a preheated oven for 25-30 minutes. Serve immediately.

• MUSHROOM AND STILTON TRICORNS •

15 g (½ oz) butter
1 small onion, peeled and chopped
75 g (3 oz) mushrooms, finely chopped
50 g (2 oz) Stilton cheese, grated
salt
freshly ground black pepper
1 small egg, beaten
100 g (4 oz) frozen puff pastry, thawed
To garnish:
sprigs of parsley

Preparation time: 15 minutes, plus chilling
Cooking time: 20-25 minutes
Oven: 220°C, 425°F, Gas Mark 7

1. Melt the butter in a small pan, add the onion and mushrooms and cook until soft. Raise the heat to evap-orate any liquid, then add the Stilton, salt, pepper and 1 tablespoon of the egg.

2. Roll out the pastry and cut into three 13 cm (5 inch) circles, rerolling the pastry if necessary.

3. Place one-third of the mushroom mixture in the centre of each pastry circle. Brush the edge of the pastry with the beaten egg, then bring up the edges of the pastry to make a three-cornered shape.

4. Brush the tricorns with beaten egg, then chill for 30 minutes. Ⓐ

5. Place in a preheated oven and cook for 15-20 minutes. Garnish and serve hot.

Ⓐ The tricorns can be made up to 1 day in advance. Keep covered and chilled.

• MARINATED AUBERGINE SALAD • ✓

1 × 225 g (8 oz) aubergine
salt
2 tablespoons olive oil
2 teaspoons white wine vinegar
1 garlic clove, peeled and crushed
1 small red pepper, cored, seeded and sliced
6 black olives
freshly ground black pepper
2 teaspoons chopped fresh parsley
To serve:
chicory leaves
sprig of parsley

Preparation time: 10 minutes, plus salting and cooling
Cooking time: 5 minutes

1. Cut the aubergine into thick slices, then again into thick sticks. Place in a colander, sprinkle with salt and leave to drain for 30 minutes. Rinse the aubergine pieces and dry with paper towels.
2. Heat the olive oil in a pan, add the aubergine and cook for 4-5 minutes, stirring frequently, until the aubergine is lightly browned.
3. Add the vinegar and garlic to the pan, bring to the boil, then transfer to a dish. Ⓐ Leave until quite cold.
4. When cold, add the red pepper, olives, salt and pepper and sprinkle with the chopped parsley.
5. Serve with chicory leaves and parsley.

Ⓐ The mixture can be prepared 1 day in advance, if kept covered and chilled, but should be served at room temperature.

FROM THE LEFT: Mushroom and Stilton tricorns, Marinated aubergine salad

• AVOCADO PEAR WALDORF • ✓

½ small avocado pear, peeled
½ small red skinned apple, cored
1 teaspoon lemon juice
1 tablespoon mayonnaise
1 celery stick, finely chopped
salt
freshly ground black pepper
1 walnut half
celery leaves, to garnish

Preparation time: 10 minutes

1. Cut the avocado and apple into thin slices lengthways. Put alternate slices on a plate. Brush with lemon juice.
2. Mix together the mayonnaise, celery, salt and pepper and place at the bottom of the avocado and apple. Top with the walnut half. Garnish and serve.

• ASPARAGUS WITH LIME MAYONNAISE •

225 g (8 oz) asparagus
1 tablespoon mayonnaise
1 teaspoon lime juice
salt
freshly ground black pepper
1 teaspoon grated lime rind
To garnish:
twists of lime
fresh dill

Preparation time: 10 minutes, plus cooling
Cooking time: 5-10 minutes

1. Trim the base of the asparagus, and cook in boiling salted water for about 5-10 minutes until the stalks are just tender. Drain well, then leave to cool. Ⓐ
2. Mix together the mayonnaise, lime juice, salt and pepper.
3. Arrange the cold asparagus on a plate, put the mayonnaise at the stalk end and sprinkle the lime rind on top of the mayonnaise.
4. Garnish and serve.

Ⓐ The asparagus can be cooked up to 1 day in advance if kept covered and chilled.

FROM THE LEFT: Avocado pear Waldorf, Asparagus with lime mayonnaise

· CAULIFLOWER WITH YOGURT, · PAPRIKA AND SUNFLOWER SEEDS

225 g (8 oz) cauliflower, cut into small florets
15 g (½ oz) butter
1 small onion, peeled and finely chopped
1 teaspoon paprika
1 tomato, skinned, seeded and chopped
1 × 150 g (5 oz) carton plain unsweetened yogurt
salt
freshly ground black pepper
To garnish:
1 teaspoon sunflower seeds
sprig of parsley

Preparation time: 10 minutes
Cooking time: 15 minutes

1. Cook the cauliflower in a pan of boiling salted water for about 5 minutes until just tender. Drain well. Ⓐ
2. Melt the butter in a pan, add the onion and cook until soft. Add the paprika and cook for 2-3 minutes. Add the tomato and cauliflower and heat gently, stirring all the time.
3. Add the yogurt to the pan and reheat, but do not boil. Season with salt and pepper.
4. Serve garnished with the sunflower seeds and parsley.

Ⓐ The cauliflower can be cooked 2-3 hours in advance, if kept covered and chilled.

· CHICORY CUSTARD ·

1 head chicory, about 175 g (6 oz)
1 egg, beaten
150 ml (¼ pint) milk
salt
freshly ground black pepper
25 g (1 oz) Cheddar cheese, grated

Preparation time: 10 minutes
Cooking time: 35 minutes
Oven: 180°C, 350°F, Gas Mark 4

This baked custard is excellent with roast meats.

1. Cut away the core from the base of the chicory and discard. Cut the chicory into thick slices, then cook in a pan of boiling salted water for 5 minutes. Drain well.
2. Mix together the egg, milk, salt, pepper and grated cheese. Add the chicory and place the mixture in a small ovenproof dish. Ⓐ
3. Place the dish in another pan, with boiling water to come halfway up the sides of the dish.
4. Place in a preheated oven and cook for about 30 minutes, until the custard has set and is lightly browned.

Ⓐ The custard can be prepared up to 1 day in advance, if kept covered and chilled.

· POMMES DE TERRE PROVENÇALES ·

1 × 175-225 g (6-8 oz) potato, peeled and thinly sliced
2 teaspoons olive oil
1 small onion, peeled and sliced
1 small garlic clove, peeled and crushed
1 medium beefsteak tomato, skinned and sliced
½ teaspoon herbes de Provence
salt
freshly ground black pepper
3 tablespoons stock
1 teaspoon butter
To garnish:
a tomato rose

Preparation time: 10 minutes
Cooking time: about 1 hour
Oven: 190°C, 375°F, Gas Mark 5,
then: 220°C, 425°F, Gas Mark 7

FROM THE LEFT: Cauliflower with yogurt, paprika and sunflower seeds, Pommes de terre Provençales

1. Place the potato slices in a pan of salted water and bring to the boil. Reduce the heat and simmer for 2-3 minutes. Drain well, then dry on paper towels.
2. Melt the oil in a small pan, add the onion and garlic and cook until softened.
3. In a small ovenproof dish, place one-third of the potato slices, half of the tomato, half of the onion and garlic mixture and half of the herbs. Repeat the layers and finish with a layer of potato on top. Season each layer of potatoes with a little salt and pepper.
4. Pour the stock over the potatoes and dot with the butter. Cover the dish with foil, place in a preheated oven and cook for 40 minutes.
5. Remove the foil from the dish, increase the oven temperature and cook for a further 10-15 minutes to brown the top of the potatoes. Garnish and serve.

• BULGHAR PILAFF • ✓

25 g (1 oz) butter
1 small bunch spring onions, chopped
50 g (2 oz) bulghar, soaked for 30 minutes
½ teaspoon ground turmeric
175-200 ml (6-7 fl oz) stock
1 carrot, peeled and diced
1 celery stick, sliced, leaves reserved
salt
freshly ground black pepper
25 g (1 oz) frozen peas

Preparation time: 10 minutes
Cooking time: 25 minutes

1. Melt the butter in a pan. Add three-quarters of the spring onion, the bulghar and turmeric and stir well. Cook gently for about 5 minutes, stirring frequently.
2. Add the stock, carrot, celery, salt and pepper to the pan. Bring to the boil, then reduce the heat, cover the pan and simmer gently for 15 minutes, stirring occasionally.
3. Add the peas to the pan and a little extra stock if the pilaff is drying out too quickly.
4. Simmer for 5 minutes more until the liquid has evaporated and the bulghar is soft and has doubled in volume.
5. Serve with the reserved spring onion and celery.

• SCALLOPED BEANS •

100 g (4 oz) cooked French beans
1 egg, hard-boiled and sliced
15 g (½ oz) butter
15 g (½ oz) flour
150 ml (¼ pint) milk
salt
freshly ground black pepper
25 g (1 oz) fresh white breadcrumbs
15 g (½ oz) Cheddar cheese, grated
To garnish:
sprig of parsley

Preparation time: 10 minutes
Cooking time: 30 minutes
Oven: 180°C, 350°F, Gas Mark 4

1. In a small ovenproof dish, layer the beans and hard-boiled egg.
2. Melt the butter in a small pan, add the flour and cook for 2-3 minutes. Add the milk to the pan and bring to the boil, stirring all the time. Cook for a further 2-3 minutes. Season with salt and pepper.
3. Pour the sauce over the beans and egg, shaking the dish gently to make sure they are thoroughly coated.

4. Sprinkle the breadcrumbs and cheese over the dish. Ⓐ
5. Place in a preheated oven and cook for about 20 minutes. Garnish and serve.

Ⓐ The dish can be prepared 2-3 hours in advance if kept covered and chilled.

Variation:
This dish is equally good prepared with 100 g (4 oz) shelled weight of broad beans.

• ROOT VEGETABLES IN PARSLEY SAUCE • ✓

1 small parsnip, peeled and cored
1 × 75 g (3 oz) piece swede, peeled
75 g (3 oz) baby carrots, peeled
85 ml (3 fl oz) reserved cooking water
15 g (½ oz) butter
15 g (½ oz) flour
50 ml (2 fl oz) single cream
1 tablespoon chopped fresh parsley
salt
freshly ground black pepper

Preparation time: 10 minutes
Cooking time: 15 minutes

1. Cut the parsnip and swede into pieces the same size as the carrots. Cook the vegetables in boiling salted water until just tender, about 5 minutes. Drain well, reserving 85 ml (3 fl oz) of the cooking water. Ⓐ
2. Melt the butter in a small pan, add the flour and cook for 2-3 minutes. Add the reserved cooking water and cream and bring to the boil, stirring all the time. Cook for a further 2-3 minutes. Add the parsley to the pan and taste and adjust the seasoning.
3. Place the drained vegetables in the sauce and reheat gently.

Ⓐ The vegetables can be cooked 2-3 hours in advance. Keep covered and chilled.

TOP: Bulghar pilaff; BOTTOM: Scalloped beans

FINISHING TOUCHES

✓ • MARBLED RASPBERRY MOUSSE •

100 g (4 oz) raspberries or blackcurrants, stewed in
150 ml (½ pint) water *or* 1 × 215 g (7½ oz) can
unsweetened raspberries or blackcurrants
1 egg (size 4), separated
2 tablespoons caster sugar
1 scant teaspoon powdered gelatine
1 tablespoon water

Preparation time: 15 minutes, plus setting

This recipe makes a very generous portion. Any leftover can be stored, covered, in the refrigerator for 2-3 days. Alternatively, divide into 2 portions when entertaining.

1. Sieve the fruit and discard the skins and seeds. Make the purée up to 120 ml (4 fl oz) with some of the juice.
2. Put the egg yolk into a bowl, add 1 tablespoon of the sugar and whisk until thick and fluffy.
3. Dissolve the gelatine in the water and add to the egg yolk mixture with the fruit purée. Chill until just beginning to set.
4. Whisk the egg white until stiff, then whisk in the remaining tablespoon of sugar.
5. Fold the egg white very lightly into the fruit mixture, leaving streaks to make a marbled effect.
6. To serve, pour into a tall stemmed glass. Chill until set.

✓ • WHITE CHOCOLATE MOUSSE •

50 g (2 oz) white chocolate
1 egg, separated
4 teaspoons double or whipping cream, whipped
To serve:
15 g (½ oz) plain chocolate, grated

Preparation time: 10 minutes, plus chilling
Cooking time: 2-3 minutes

1. Melt the chocolate in a basin over a pan of hot water. Remove from the heat and cool slightly, then add the egg yolk and half of the cream.
2. Whisk the egg white until stiff and fold into the chocolate mixture. Transfer to a small glass bowl, then place in the refrigerator for 2-3 hours to set.
3. To serve, top the mousse with the remaining cream and sprinkle with the grated plain chocolate.

✓ • PINK GRAPEFRUIT JELLY •

1 pink grapefruit
1 tablespoon caster sugar
4 tablespoons water
2 teaspoons powdered gelatine
2 drops pink food colouring

Preparation time: 10 minutes, plus chilling

1. Cut the grapefruit horizontally three-quarters of the way down into 2 pieces.
2. Squeeze the juice from both pieces, then carefully remove the pith, squeezing out any remaining juice.
3. Discard the smaller piece of skin. Wash the larger piece and dry thoroughly. Cut the edge in a zig-zag, if wished.
4. Place the sugar in a small pan with 2 tablespoons of water and heat until the sugar has dissolved. Add the syrup to the grapefruit juice.
5. Dissolve the gelatine in the remaining water over a low heat, then add to the grapefruit juice with the pink food colouring. Stir well.
6. Place the reserved grapefruit skin in a small dish to keep it upright, then strain the grapefruit juice into it. Chill for 2-3 hours until set.

CLOCKWISE FROM THE TOP: Pink grapefruit jelly, White chocolate mousse, Marbled raspberry mousse

✓ · PRUNE AND YOGURT WHIP ·

1 × 225 g (8 oz) can prunes, drained and stoned
1 × 150 g (5 oz) carton plain unsweetened yogurt
1 teaspoon brandy (optional)
1 egg white
To decorate:
1 teaspoon toasted flaked almonds

Preparation time: 10 minutes

1. Cut the prunes into small pieces. Mix them with the yogurt and brandy, if using.
2. Whisk the egg white until stiff, then fold into the yogurt mixture.
3. Pour into a stemmed glass and decorate with the flaked almonds.

· PINEAPPLE CUSTARD CREAM · ✔

1 teaspoon golden syrup
1 slice canned pineapple in syrup
1 egg
85 ml (3 fl oz) milk
50 ml (2 fl oz) pineapple syrup from can
1 tcaspoon caster sugar
To decorate:
1 yellow glacé cherry
2 angelica diamonds

Preparation time: 5 minutes, plus cooling
Cooking time: 30 minutes

Unsweetened pineapple can be used if an extra teaspoon of caster sugar is added in step 2.

1. Spread the golden syrup over the base of a ramekin dish. Place the pineapple slice on top.
2. Mix together the egg, milk, pineapple syrup and sugar. Strain the mixture over the top of the pineapple slice. Cover the dish with foil.
3. Place the dish in a small frying pan. Pour boiling water in the pan to come halfway up the side of the dish. Cover the pan and simmer gently for 30 minutes.
4. Check the pan from time to time and add more boiling water if necessary to maintain the level.
5. When cooked, remove the dish from the pan, cool, then turn out on to a serving dish.
6. Decorate and serve cold.

· INDIVIDUAL ALASKA ·

1 trifle sponge or 2 thin slices of jam Swiss roll
2 teaspoons sherry
1 individual block vanilla ice cream
50 g (2 oz) loganberries or blackberries
1 egg white
25 g (1 oz) caster sugar

Preparation time: 10 minutes
Cooking time: 2-3 minutes
Oven: 230°C, 450°F, Gas Mark 8

1. Cut the trifle sponge in half horizontally. Place the trifle sponge or Swiss roll in a small shallow ovenproof dish. Sprinkle with the sherry.
2. Place the ice cream on top of the cake and pile the fruit on top.
3. Whisk the egg white until stiff, then whisk in the caster sugar until the mixture is stiff and glossy.
4. Pipe or spread the meringue over the fruit and ice cream, making sure that they are completely covered.
5. Place in a preheated oven for 2-3 minutes, to brown the meringue. Serve immediately.

FROM THE LEFT: Pineapple custard cream, Individual Alaska

· STRAWBERRIES WITH FROMAGE · BLANC

100 g (4 oz) fromage blanc
1 tablespoon caster sugar
few drops of vanilla essence
75 g (3 oz) strawberries, wiped and hulled
To decorate:
sprig of lemon balm

Preparation time: 5 minutes

1. Mix together the fromage blanc, three-quarters of the caster sugar and the vanilla essence. Place in a shallow glass dish.
2. Place the strawberries on top of the fromage blanc and sprinkle with the remaining caster sugar.
3. Decorate and serve.

· KIWI SABAYON ·

1 egg yolk
1 tablespoon caster sugar
2 tablespoons sweet white wine or sherry
1 kiwi fruit, peeled and sliced
To decorate:
few kiwi slices

Preparation time: 5 minutes
Cooking time: 10 minutes

1. Place the egg yolk, sugar and wine in a bowl and mix well together.
2. Place the bowl over a pan of simmering water and whisk constantly until the mixture is light and thick and has doubled in volume.
3. Place the slices of kiwi fruit on a small shallow dish. Pour the egg yolk mixture over the fruit. Place the dish under a preheated hot grill and cook for 1-2 minutes until the top is browned.
4. Decorate and serve.

FROM THE LEFT: Strawberries with fromage blanc, Kiwi sabayon

• BAKED APPLE SOUFFLÉ •

1 × 225 g (8 oz) cooking apple
25 g (1 oz) caster sugar
1 tablespoon water
1 egg (size 4), separated

Preparation time: 10 minutes
Cooking time: 45 minutes
Oven: 160°C, 325°F, Gas Mark 3

1. Cut the apple in half horizontally. Remove most of the flesh from the apple, leaving 2 thin shells.
2. Sprinkle a little sugar around each apple shell. Discard the apple core, then put the flesh into a small pan with the remaining sugar and water.
3. Simmer until soft, then increase the heat and cook until the purée is quite dry.
4. Allow the purée to cool slightly, then add the egg yolk.
5. Whisk the egg white until stiff, then fold into the apple purée.
6. Pile the purée into the apple shells. Place the shells in a small ovenproof dish and bake in a preheated oven for 40 minutes. Serve immediately.

✓ • BANANA AND ORANGE CRUMBLE •

1 large banana
2 tablespoons orange juice
1 teaspoon grated orange rind
1 tablespoon caster sugar
25 g (1 oz) butter
25 g (1 oz) plain flour
25 g (1 oz) soft brown sugar
25 g (1 oz) chopped walnuts
To decorate:
slices of orange

Preparation time: 10 minutes
Cooking time: 25 minutes
Oven: 190°C, 375°F, Gas Mark 5

1. Cut the banana into thick slices. Mix with the orange juice, rind and sugar then place in a small ovenproof dish.
2. In a mixing bowl, rub the butter into the flour until the mixture resembles fine breadcrumbs. Add the sugar and walnuts, then sprinkle the crumble topping over the bananas.
3. Place in a preheated oven and cook for 25 minutes. Decorate and serve hot.

A crumble is a very versatile pudding. Try making it with rhubarb and a sprinkling of ground ginger, or plums and a little ground cinnamon. The walnuts can be substituted with flaked almonds or chopped hazelnuts.

• PEAR POACHED WITH HONEY, • LEMON AND GINGER

1 tablespoon clear honey
1 teaspoon grated lemon rind
1 tablespoon lemon juice
¼ teaspoon ground ginger
120 ml (4 fl oz) water
1 pear, peeled, cored and cut into quarters
To decorate:
twist of lemon rind

Preparation time: 5 minutes, plus cooling
Cooking time: 20 minutes

FROM THE LEFT: Banana and orange crumble, Pear poached with honey, lemon and ginger

1. Put the honey, lemon rind and juice, ginger and water into a pan and bring to the boil.
2. Add the pear to the pan, cover and simmer for 15 minutes, until the pear is tender.
3. Put the pear on to a small serving dish. Boil up the liquid in the pan until reduced to about 2 tablespoons. Pour the reduced liquid over the pear and leave to go cold.
4. Decorate with lemon and serve with cream.

• BREAD AND BUTTERSCOTCH •
PUDDING

25 g (1 oz) butter
25 g (1 oz) soft brown sugar
85 ml (3 fl oz) single cream
50 ml (2 fl oz) milk
1 small egg, beaten
2 thin slices white bread, crusts removed
25 g (1 oz) sultanas

Preparation time: 10 minutes
Cooking time: 35 minutes
Oven: 180°C, 350°F, Gas Mark 4

1. Place the butter, sugar and cream in a small saucepan and heat gently until the butter and sugar have melted. Bring to the boil, stirring all the time, until the mixture becomes syrupy.
2. Add the milk and beaten egg, then mix well.
3. Cut the bread into fingers and place half of the bread in a

FROM THE LEFT: Brandy snaps filled with syllabub, Hazelnut and chocolate cookies

• BRANDY SNAPS FILLED WITH • SYLLABUB

85 ml (3 fl oz) double cream
2 teaspoons caster sugar
1 teaspoon grated lemon rind
1 teaspoon lemon juice
1 teaspoon grated orange rind
2 teaspoons orange juice
3 small brandy snaps

Preparation time: 10 minutes

1. Whisk the cream until stiff, then add the sugar, lemon rind and juice, and orange rind and juice. Whisk again until the mixture thickens.
2. Fill each brandy snap with one-third of the syllabub and serve immediately.

• HAZELNUT AND CHOCOLATE • COOKIES

75 g (3 oz) soft margarine
75 g (3 oz) granulated sugar
75 g (3 oz) soft brown sugar
1 egg, size 4
175 g (6 oz) self-raising flour, sieved
50 g (2 oz) hazelnuts, toasted and chopped
margarine, for greasing
50 g (2 oz) plain chocolate

Preparation time: 10 minutes
Cooking time: 20 minutes
Oven: 180°C, 350°F, Gas Mark 4

small ovenproof dish. Sprinkle with half of the sultanas and pour half of the butterscotch sauce over. Repeat the layers. A
4. Place in a preheated oven and cook for 30 minutes.

A The pudding can be prepared 2-3 hours in advance. Keep covered and chilled.

1. Place the margarine, sugars, egg, flour and hazelnuts in a bowl and mix thoroughly.
2. Drop teaspoonfuls of the mixture on to well greased baking sheets, allowing room for them to spread.
3. Place in a preheated oven and cook for 15 minutes. Remove to a wire tray to cool.
4. Melt the chocolate in a basin over a pan of hot water. When the cookies are quite cold, drizzle or pipe a little melted chocolate over each one with a teaspoon.

• HONEY AND SPICE BISCUITS •

75 g (3 oz) plain flour
½ teaspoon bicarbonate of soda
50 g (2 oz) caster sugar
75 g (3 oz) rolled oats
1 teaspoon mixed spice
75 g (3 oz) butter or hard margarine
2 tablespoons clear honey
1 tablespoon milk
butter or margarine, for greasing

Preparation time: 10 minutes
Cooking time: 30-35 minutes
Oven: 160°C, 325°F, Gas Mark 3

1. Sift the flour and bicarbonate of soda into a bowl. Add the sugar, rolled oats and mixed spice, then mix well.
2. Place the butter or margarine, honey and milk in a small pan and heat gently until melted.
3. Mix the honey mixture with the dry ingredients and stir thoroughly.
4. Drop teaspoonfuls of the mixture on to well greased baking sheets. Flatten the mounds slightly with the back of the spoon.
5. Place in a preheated oven and bake for 25-30 minutes. Cool on a wire tray. Serve cold.
6. Store in an airtight tin.

Cakes and biscuits made for one should be quick and easy to prepare and should keep well. Store them in an airtight tin or wrapped first in greaseproof paper, then in foil. Both the Hazelnut and chocolate cookies (page 75) and the Honey and spice biscuits (above) keep well in an airtight tin. Cakes made with oil, such as the Pineapple and brazil nut cake (opposite), stay particularly moist. This is a good basic cake recipe: the pineapple and brazil nuts can be substituted with dried fruits and other nuts, for example, dates and walnuts or apricots and almonds.

Both the Earl Grey fruit cake and the Herb and cheese quick bread (page 79) will keep for 3-4 days in an airtight tin. After that, serve them toasted and buttered.

The Sesame and blue cheese thins (page 79) are delicious both on their own and served with soups or dips. The blue cheese can be replaced by any other hard cheese, and finely-chopped nuts can be used instead of the sesame seeds.

TOP: Pineapple and brazil nut cake: BOTTOM: Peach and oatmeal fingers

• PINEAPPLE AND BRAZIL NUT CAKE •

2 eggs
175 g (6 oz) soft brown sugar
150 ml (5 fl oz) oil
1 × 225 g (8 oz) can crushed pineapple, drained
225 g (8 oz) plain flour
1 teaspoon baking powder
50 g (2 oz) brazil nuts, chopped
oil, for greasing

Preparation time: 10 minutes
Cooking time: 1 hour
Oven: 160°C, 325°F, Gas Mark 3

1. Place the eggs, sugar, oil and crushed pineapple in a bowl and mix well.
2. Sift in the flour and baking powder and fold into the mixture. Stir in the brazil nuts.
3. Put the mixture into a greased and lined 18 cm (7 inch) cake tin. Place in a preheated oven and cook for 1 hour. Turn out on to a wire tray to cool completely.

• PEACH AND OATMEAL FINGERS •

100 g (4 oz) butter or hard margarine
100 g (4 oz) caster sugar
100 g (4 oz) self-raising flour
pinch of bicarbonate of soda
100 g (4 oz) rolled oats
1 egg, beaten
butter or margarine, for greasing
2 ripe peaches, skinned and sliced

Preparation time: 15 minutes
Cooking time: 40-45 minutes
Oven: 190°C, 375°F, Gas Mark 5

When fresh peaches are not in season, this recipe can be made with well drained canned peaches.

1. Melt the butter or margarine in a pan. Add the sugar and stir well until the sugar has melted.
2. Sift in the flour and bicarbonate of soda, then stir in the rolled oats.
3. Cool the mixture slightly, then beat in the egg.
4. Grease and line an 18 cm (7 inch) square cake tin. Place half of the cake mixture in the tin and arrange the peaches on top, pressing the slices down lightly. Top with the remaining mixture, spreading it gently over the peaches.
5. Place in a preheated oven and cook for 35-40 minutes. Cool slightly in the tin, then cut into fingers. Transfer to a wire tray to cool.

• SESAME AND BLUE CHEESE THINS •

50 g (2 oz) plain flour
50 g (2 oz) butter
50 g (2 oz) blue cheese, finely grated
butter, for greasing
1 egg yolk, beaten with a pinch of salt
1 tablespoon sesame seeds

Preparation time: 10 minutes, plus chilling
Cooking time: 10 minutes
Oven: 200°C, 400°F, Gas Mark 6

1. Sieve the flour into a bowl and rub in the butter until the mixture resembles fine breadcrumbs. Stir in the cheese, then gather the mixture up into a ball. Wrap in cling film and chill for about 30 minutes. Ⓐ
2. Roll out the dough between 2 sheets of cling film. Cut the dough into shapes – hearts, triangles, etc. – and reroll the trimmings.
3. Place the shapes on to a greased baking sheet. Brush with the egg yolk and sprinkle with the sesame seeds.
4. Place in a preheated oven and cook for 10 minutes. Transfer to a wire tray to cool.

Ⓐ The dough can be prepared up to 1 day in advance. Keep chilled.

• HERB AND CHEESE QUICK BREAD •

225 g (8 oz) self-raising flour
1 teaspoon salt
100 g (4 oz) soft margarine, at room temperature
200 ml (7 fl oz) buttermilk
1 egg, beaten
100 g (4 oz) Sage Derby cheese, grated
margarine, for greasing

Preparation time: 10 minutes
Cooking time: 50-55 minutes
Oven: 190°C, 375°F, Gas Mark 5

1. Sift the flour and salt into a bowl. Add the margarine, buttermilk and egg and mix well.
2. Add most of the cheese, reserving 1 tablespoon. Put the mixture into a well-greased 450 g (1 lb) loaf tin. Sprinkle the reserved cheese over the top.
3. Place in a preheated oven and bake for 50-55 minutes. Remove from the oven and leave in the tin until almost cold. Transfer to a wire tray to finish cooling.
4. Serve sliced and buttered.

• EARL GREY FRUIT CAKE •

50 g (2 oz) sultanas
50 g (2 oz) raisins
50 g (2 oz) currants
1 teaspoon grated lemon rind
100 g (4 oz) demerara sugar
150 ml (¼ pint) cold strong Earl Grey tea, strained
1 egg, beaten
225 g (8 oz) self-raising flour
butter or margarine, for greasing

Preparation time: 10 minutes, plus soaking overnight
Cooking time: 1 hour
Oven: 160°C, 325°F, Gas Mark 3

Fruit cakes such as this one rely on dried fruits for their full-bodied flavour. They need no further decoration.

1. Place the sultanas, raisins and currants in a bowl. Add the lemon rind and all but 1 teaspoon of the demerara sugar. Pour the strained tea over the top, mix well, then cover and leave until the next day to enable the tea to be absorbed into the dried fruit and sugar.
2. Add the beaten egg to the dried fruit mixture and combine well.
3. Sift the flour into the mixture and fold in gently with a metal spoon.
4. Place the mixture in a greased and lined 500 g (1¼ lb) loaf tin. Sprinkle with the reserved demerara sugar.
5. Place in a preheated oven and bake for about 1 hour. Turn out on to a wire tray to cool. Ⓐ
6. Cut the cake into slices when serving.

Ⓐ The cake will keep for 3-4 days in an airtight tin. After this time, serve it toasted and buttered.

CLOCKWISE FROM THE TOP: Sesame and blue cheese thins, Earl Grey fruit cake, Herb and cheese quick bread

INDEX